WATCHDOG

WATCHDOG

CONGRESSMAN
DARRELL ISSA

CENTER
STREET®

NEW YORK   BOSTON   NASHVILLE

For my father, William Issa, whose

work ethic I closely studied, tried to emulate,

and have yet to in any way equal.

Center Street
Hachette Book Group
1290 Avenue of the Americas, New York, NY 10104
centerstreet.com
twitter.com/centerstreet

First Edition: July 2016

Center Street is a division of Hachette Book Group, Inc. The Center Street name and logo are trademarks of Hachette Book Group, Inc.

The publisher is not responsible for websites (or their content) that are not owned by the publisher.

The Hachette Speakers Bureau provides a wide range of authors for speaking events. To find out more, go to www.HachetteSpeakersBureau.com or call (866) 376-6591.

Print book interior design by Timothy Shaner, nightanddaydesign.biz

Library of Congress Cataloging-in-Publication Data has been applied for.

ISBNs: 978-1-4555-9198-5 (hardcover), 978-1-4555-9196-1 (ebook)

Printed in the United States of America

RRD-C

10 9 8 7 6 5 4 3 2 1

CONTENTS

1. How We Got Here 1

2. The Big Obstacle: Big Government 7

3. The Answer: Transparency, Accountability, and Reform . . .17

4. A Life before Government 21

5. From Business Veteran to Government Rookie 55

6. The Recall Election and the Rise of the Terminator 79

7. Second Thoughts on Six Years with the Fourth Estate . . . 91

8. Fast and Furious 107

9. The Difference Benghazi Makes 125

10. Lois Lerner: The Power to Tax and the Power to Destroy. . .141

11. Hillary's Got a Secret (Email Server) 157

12. Bank Accounts as Political Weapons 169

13. Bank Bailouts: Exposed but Unstoppable 179

14. Turning a Deaf Ear to Whistle-blowers and
a Blind Eye to Cover-ups 191

15. Why the Oversight Committee Keeps Watch 201

16. Taking the Administration to Court 217

17. The Only Good Government Is Open Government 225

18. Looking Back, Moving Ahead 233

Acknowledgments 241

Endnotes 243

We exist to secure two fundamental principles. First, Americans have a right to know that the money Washington takes from them is well spent. And second, Americans deserve an efficient, effective government that works for them. Our duty on the Oversight and Government Reform Committee is to protect these rights.

Our solemn responsibility is to hold government accountable to taxpayers, because taxpayers have a right to know what they get from their government. We will work tirelessly, in partnership with citizen-watchdogs, to deliver the facts to the American people and bring genuine reform to the federal bureaucracy.

—Mission Statement of the House Committee
on Oversight and Government Reform

CHAPTER ONE

How We Got Here

Something has gone terribly wrong in our national conception of governmental power, public accountability, and the American people's right to access what the government knows and have the strongest voice in impacting what it does.

From as far back as our Founders and right up until today, these bedrock values have represented the core of our republic, bolstered our enduring democracy, and called to account the men and women who stand for election, ask for the voters' trust, and serve as the people's representatives. This is also the story of the merits of transparency and its role in our government at all levels—allowing the people to see, shape, and understand a democracy that is, ultimately, theirs and theirs alone.

As our government has grown, so, too, has its influence over and connection to nearly every aspect of our lives. In the process, it has extracted a steep price from the people it is sworn to serve that cannot be measured even in the trillions of dollars. Today, government now knows far more about its people, while the people seem to know less and less about their government. As Washington's power has intensified, it has also given us more to fight about, more reason to argue, and driven us further apart.

This has also created a crisis of confidence in the presidency, the Congress, the bureaucracy, even our laws. Every American should worry about this. I hope every American will want to change it. But if government cannot even launch a functional website of the president's signature social goal of his health care plan—let alone balance the federal books and shrink the national debt—public cynicism will only rise.

It's not enough just to rage against this reality. A better way is to open up the system to the people and let information and access flow at the speed of light. Let's reveal as much of government as we can to as many people as possible, every chance we get. We need to give people not only an understanding of what government does but access to what government knows and restore the principle that public information is neither a hindrance nor a nuisance

Then—and only then—can Congress, the White House, or the massive federal system truly claim to have the consent of the governed.

We need to provide a better way to test and limit the power of Washington. For fifteen years, I've seen the best this capital has to offer, particularly at those times when we were trying to fix what was most wrong with it. For ten years, I served as a member of the House Committee on Oversight and Government Reform, the last four as chairman (though it probably seemed like forty to some of my Democrat colleagues).

This was a front-row seat to the tragic shortcomings of government as an institution and the disastrous choices made by an administration that has done special damage to its credibility and reputation. Barack Obama may have entered office promising hope and change, but his largely failed presidency will leave in its wake bitterness and division from coast to coast and most everywhere in between.

We did not seek to damage the Obama administration or negatively impact its standing among a majority of Americans. The actions of the White House did that. We only shone the light on what they did and what they were doing.

I am hopeful that the impact we made and the legacy we leave will extend far beyond these difficult years for our country. This book showcases brave, intrepid people and the tireless work they did, as in "watching the watchmen" and policing the powerful—following the trail of the truth wherever it took them and fighting back against inappropriate secrecy.

Sometimes that path led us to the inner sanctums of the Department of Justice, the State Department, the Pentagon, the IRS—even the White House. Other times, following the facts brought us to the offices of colleagues and even the front doors of friends. But we did not turn away.

This is also a story of good people engaged in a great calling—some anonymously, all courageously. For four years, the men and women of the Oversight Committee I chaired—members of Congress and staff alike—worked endless hours, scouring roomfuls of documents and weeks' worth of transcripts.

For four years, they withstood harsh attacks from the White House, a hostile press, and a war of words that often lasted into and through the night. For four years, they endured scorn and scowls from colleagues on the other side of the aisle—and even the disdain of many Republican friends.

We may have faced taunts from the president, opposition from the Democrats, and even obstruction from fellow Republicans, but it does not mean we stood alone. Almost every day that we investigated serial scandals in Washington and secretive wrongdoing in the executive branch, we were bolstered by supportive notes and uplifting calls from people all over the country—everyday Americans we would never know or even meet.

Many cheered us on. Others wondered what was taking so long. A few even volunteered to help. All those voices encouraged us to be dogged and determined, especially during the many times it would have been so easy to quit, drop the issue, close the book—or do a friend a favor. But we couldn't do that. So we pressed on. When you get elected to Congress, you take an oath. And when you volunteer to serve on the Oversight Committee, you pledge to transcend politics and party. At least you try. We've all fallen short before.

There is one group of people that deserves special mention: we owe a special debt to the whistle-blowers who came forward to tell the truth and in doing so risked all—and often lost much—because they possessed a sense of duty. This is their story, too.

One question I was asked more often than any other was: Why are you doing this? I never had the ideal response, because the answer seemed so obvious. We were watchdogs. We learned of wrongdoing in government and tried to reveal it. We found corruption and tried to expose it. We investigated the targeting of innocent Americans and tried to stop it.

This is also, though, the story of a life—my life. Mine is not a heroic story or even a terribly atypical one. It is a story combining the pride of immigrant heritage and immersion in what Ronald Reagan called the "American Experiment." It's a story also of midwestern values and a California dream. Of hard work and good fortune. Of a passion for innovation and desire to challenge the status quo. Of relentless discovery and continued blessings. Of service to country and service in Congress. Of looking for a way to have an impact and joining in a search for the truth.

If you can't change America for the better in Congress, you can't do it anywhere.

It should be left to others and to the judgment of history to decide if we succeeded. But I know in my heart that within this book is a presentation of events and occurrences that reveal an administration, executive branch, and federal government that exceeded their authority, abused their power, hid from accountability, and fought the public's right to know. That's why we did it. This is that story.

CHAPTER TWO

The Big Obstacle: Big Government

Good and bad actions within politics have often been done by substantially the same people, not by separate armies of saints and sinners.

Much of the bad behavior in Congress is small and inconsequential, though perhaps revealing of the mind-set of power brokers. There are the minor legends about members who require a car and driver to go one and a half blocks to work or the member who failed to board planes by their intended departure times so often that eventually one flight crew removed her luggage and asked her to consider another airline for all future flights.

Congress is an esteemed and magnificent institution, but also at times like a fraternity you never intended to rush.

I have been honored to travel to distant parts of the world with wise elder statesmen such as the late Representative Henry Hyde, a thinker and orator comparable to any of the great Supreme Court justices. But some of my colleagues in Congress have also brought shame upon themselves and the institution we serve.

The history of Congress is found in hallowed halls and revered documents—but also in Louisiana Representative William Jefferson's freezer, where he stashed some $90,000 in bribes (giving new meaning to the term "cold hard cash").

It's also found in the "bribery menu" prepared and kept by my fellow Californian Representative Randall "Duke" Cunningham. His district was adjacent to mine; I knew him well and considered him a friend. He started out a hero—a "top gun" pilot and flight instructor—but then developed a vast sense of entitlement and eventually pled guilty to accepting more than $2.4 million in bribes.

Both Cunningham and Jefferson had power, professional standing, and annual salaries many times over those of the average American. But they gave all that away, wound up in disgrace, and eventually did time in federal prison.

Too, there are the far more routine instances of perfectly legal overlap between massive public expenditures and closely related private-sector jobs, such as former Representative Billy Tauzin helping to craft the Medicare Part D subsidy for prescription medications—and promptly going to head the pharmaceutical industry lobbying group PhRMA upon his departure from Congress in 2005.

Think how helpful all those who pass through the revolving door can be to a select few. As one of my most trusted confidants, former Oversight Committee Staff Director Larry Brady, puts it, members of Congress and executive-branch appointees don't come to DC wondering what their next job will be and how much money they'll make at it—but after a few years, some do begin to think about it.

There is, of course, good and bad in any institution—and in each individual. The Founders created a nation that treasured liberty, but also owned slaves. They were antimonarchy but also suggested that the first American president travel in a gilded carriage and be addressed as "Your Majesty." Was that a sign of temptations to come? Thank goodness George Washington suggested the modest salutation still used today: Mr. President.

I do not deny that the office of the president, by tradition, is rightly shown great deference by both the Congress and the courts. Teddy Roosevelt, for example, was essentially correct to think that he had the right as president to send the navy wherever he chose, with Congress periodically exercising the power of the purse strings, not the power of micromanagement, if it concludes the president has abused his authority. The goal of this book is not to weaken current or future presidents, nor to tilt the balance of power toward this or any future Congress.

If our president is to be a respected and effective commander in chief at home and first ambassador to a troubled world, even if he sometimes makes mistakes, the office must truly be seated with great powers—but those powers cannot, and should not, be unchecked.

If even some of the most esteemed figures in our history could not be fully trusted with the power of government, surely the current crop of politicians deserves the same or more scrutiny. Our nation's founders set the three branches of government in opposition, each a check on the others, as a bulwark against tyranny. But the massive growth of the executive branch has tilted the scale heavily in its favor, exposing all Americans to its excesses and abuses.

Safeguarding freedom for the next generations will depend upon employing strong and sensible restraints on the growing executive branch that are not dependent upon the whims or personalities of any Washington politician. They must endure beyond the debates of today.

*   *   *

An important step toward restoring balance and reducing the run-away charity-like spending power of Congress is to shine a light on some of its most flawed practices. I've lost count of the number of times we have been asked to vote on massive spending bills that almost none of my colleagues has completely read or fully under-stands. That's why I support the concept of a two-year budget cycle to at least give members of Congress, as well as the American peo-ple, a greatly enhanced ability to understand and impact the way in which trillions of dollars are being spent. The public has a right to know what the government is doing, and the truth is, we have much to learn from public input.

But we must go beyond just managing money. We must restore trust. The Oversight Committee has a rich and honorable history in bringing hard truths to the public's view.

Oversight is crucial, since government cannot be trusted always to do the right thing. Ideally, the Speaker of the House and Congress as a whole could bring contempt charges or other legal remedies to bear on the executive branch—or could, if they possessed the cour-age, be bolstered by legislation reaffirming that power. The Over-sight Committee, by contrast, currently has only the ability to show what's wrong, not to punish anyone for it.

But showing what's wrong is not being silent about it. That's why the oversight function can make a difference.

For example, Harry Truman's leadership of a Senate commit-tee to investigate wasteful military spending made him a prominent figure leading up to his selection as Franklin D. Roosevelt's final vice presidential running mate. In the late 1950s, Robert F. Kennedy first butted heads with Teamsters leader Jimmy Hoffa while serving as chief counsel and investigator of a select congressional commit-tee looking into corrupt union practices.

One of my own predecessors as chairman of the Oversight Committee was Representative Dan Burton (R-IN), who permanently altered the public perception of Al Gore by drawing attention to illegal campaign contributions the Clinton-Gore campaign had received from Buddhist monks who had clearly not taken vows of poverty.

Sometimes we even need oversight of the people who are supposed to be doing oversight, as when the committee, under the chairmanship of Representative Tom Davis (R-VA), exposed gross mismanagement and incompetence at the Mineral Management Service (MMS), which was tasked with leasing federal lands to gas and oil companies.

When Congress changed hands and Democrat Henry Waxman assumed the chair, he terminated our investigation, preferring to scrutinize businesses and industries he was unsympathetic to, rather than wrongdoing in the government and the public sector. I often wondered where the "G" in the OGR Committee went during his tenure.

He should have kept the focus on Washington, for he found himself embarrassed months later when an inspector general reported that MMS staffers had abused drugs and had affairs with members of the industries they were supposed to be keeping an eye on and from which they were supposed to be collecting royalties for the benefit of the taxpayers.

The irresponsibility of the MMS would become even more costly during its inept handling of events preceding the BP oil spill. How could there be so little blame placed on the government bureaucracy whose inspectors had given the rig an OK, had specified the location and manner of the drilling in so much regulatory detail, and had approved changes in the BP well's design that might have contributed to its failure?

I believe that if Waxman had not cast aside our investigation while it was still ongoing, there would have been a far greater likelihood of rooting out some of the real troubles in the MMS so it could have performed its duties and helped to prevent the BP oil spill.

But that didn't happen, another example of the fact that executive-branch bureaucrats are almost never fired—and almost never even known to the public by name. Congress rarely takes them to task, and, as a consequence, they tend to act as if they are beyond the reach of accountability. The MMS sure did.

There are also vast waste and corruption even in those few parts of government that conservatives support, including the military— and as an army veteran who rose to the rank of captain, this is a troubling truth. Congress was right to take the Pentagon to task for the essentially indiscriminate distribution of money in war-torn Iraq in which the United States essentially dropped bales of cash all over that nation in the desperate hope of winning local favor and jump-starting its economy.

Why was anyone surprised when corruption occurred?

More recently, the Oversight Committee brought to public awareness a true Washington spending scandal that engulfed, ironically, the General Services Association (GSA), which is charged with spending and purchasing for the federal government.

At a Las Vegas conference that was already unnecessary, the GSA spent $130,000 for preconference "scouting"; $75,000 on a bike-building training exercise; $19 per person for an "American artisanal cheese display"; $7,000 for sushi; $3,200 for a mind reader; $3,700 for T-shirts; and more than $2,500 on bottled water.

The Huffington Post reported that agency personnel also staged a parody video production of an awards show red-carpet entrance into a conference room gathering, during which GSA officials discussed the expensive, stylish designer clothes they were wearing. The acting GSA administrator at the time, Jeff Neely, who reports found encouraged organizers to make sure the conference was "over the top," described his outfit as totally Armani.

My personal favorite was a video filmed especially for the conference—inside GSA headquarters—featuring an employee playing a ukulele and singing a homespun ode to binge-spending culture and an office shopping spree on the taxpayers' dime.

Why was anyone surprised when corruption occurred there?

Much of what was discovered at the GSA was the result of an internal investigation by the agency's inspector general. That was good. What was troubling was the revelation that the GSA inspector general had briefed the Obama administration almost a year prior to the revelations about its findings of waste and wrongdoing at the lavish Las Vegas convention.

Rather than taking immediate action to suspend or dismiss those identified as responsible, the Obama administration instead let them have bonuses and took real personnel actions only when there were no more options for delay. It wouldn't be the last time that would occur.

Most of the time, though, we don't have embarrassing videos to tell the true story. So the Oversight Committee, with a staff of about eighty, can only present the truth and expose those agents of the executive branch who refuse to respond to its subpoenas and who decline to appear at the committee's hearings. We can't arrest wrongdoers or order bureaucrats who resist our subpoenas to be jailed. Our government desperately needs more, and more aggressive, oversight if we are to protect the American people from a bureaucracy with too much power and little accountability.

Government gets even the most practical, basic things wrong, as the rollout of the HealthCare.gov website revealed. Until very recently, chief information officers (CIOs) within the federal government, tasked with overseeing the government's computer systems, had little real power to ensure that the latest, most cost-effective and efficient technology is used—despite a long list of failed government computer systems, of which the first version of HealthCare.gov was only one unusually high profile example.

With the passage into law of the Federal Information Technology Acquisition Reform Act, which I authored, at least now CIOs will wield the power of the purse. During the HealthCare.gov rollout, by contrast, the CIOs claimed that they lacked the authority to intervene, and the evidence showed that their recommendations and objections were ignored or overruled by agency administrators who had little or no technological know-how. Whereas private sector entities arise, evolve, and fade away in response to market signals about what works and what doesn't, government agencies keep on failing and paying little or no price for it.

In response, I cosponsored what became the Digital Account-ability and Transparency Act (DATA) in 2014. It provides more financial information about government expenditures online, and in a standardized, comprehensible fashion. But even that faced an uphill battle.

To his credit, Vice President Joe Biden expressed enthusiasm for DATA but said he was chastised for meeting with me by President Obama's "Chicago crowd." In the end, the DATA Act passed the Congress overwhelmingly, and President Obama followed up on that momentum by signing it into law.

But the real challenge to reform comes not from Democrats or

Republicans but from the established bureaucracy, which resists transparency and reform. In response, the last decade saw some important steps taken toward empowering the legislature to take the executive branch to task.

Chief among them, arguably, have been then–House Judiciary Committee Chairman Representative John Conyers (D-MI) bringing contempt of Congress charges against Bush White House Counsel Harriet Miers and Chief of Staff Joshua Bolten for their refusal to appear to testify about a mass firing of US attorneys. Another was the Oversight Committee's partial success during my chairmanship in forcing the release by the Department of Justice of documents related to its "Fast and Furious" gun-running scandal. Also important was the passage by the House, thanks to Representative Trey Gowdy (R-SC) and then-Speaker John Boehner (R-OH), of the ENFORCE the Law Act of 2014, affirming Congress's standing to sue the president.

I believe we should give individual members of Congress standing to sue agencies for information necessary for the members to fulfill their representational duties. Agencies now often treat requests for information from rank-and-file members as little more than Freedom of Information Act (FOIA) requests, but those members are responsible for approving funding for every agency and program of the federal government. How can they be expected to legislate without access to information to evaluate the performance of the programs? Giving them immediate access to the courts, to compel the immediate production of information related to matters before Congress, would produce better-informed lawmaking.

Oversight, after all, is not just about highlighting past abuses but, we hope, about preventing future ones.

CHAPTER THREE

The Answer: Transparency, Accountability, and Reform

Our political problems, then, are deep, systemic ones that cannot be solved through simple partisanship. The economist Arthur Laffer, a friend to me and a hero to many conservatives, considers Presidents Johnson, Nixon, Ford, and Carter "the Four Stooges: the largest assemblage of bipartisan ignorance ever put on planet Earth." What he means is that the power and reach of government flourished with both Republicans and Democrats in the White House, with a GOP president signing on to the creation of the Environmental Protection Agency.

In addition, the usual bland calls for "bipartisanship" don't solve anything. Indeed, between some parts of government, such as those performing oversight and those being criticized, there *ought* to be an adversarial relationship.

Where members of Congress must be united, though, is when an administration resists congressional oversight. Members can disagree about whether an administration should be investigated, but when a committee of Congress issues a subpoena, any division between the parties about whether compliance is required diminishes the effectiveness of congressional oversight and the ability of the legislature to check abuses of the executive. Laws require compliance, and both parties have an interest in enforcing congressional subpoenas with the full power of that branch.

There are many historical precedents for Congress acting as a unified body to rein in executive overreach, but modern political practice dictates that the president's party in Congress plays defense, attacking oversight to blunt its effectiveness. My Democrat counterpart, ranking member Elijah Cummings, played the role of defense counsel with great zeal (the most senior member of the minority party on a committee is known as ranking member, leads the minority party's efforts, controls a third of the staff and budget for a committee, and is the counterpart of the committee chair).

Cummings closely coordinated efforts to defeat congressional oversight with officials in the Obama White House—a role he was handpicked for by Democrat leader Nancy Pelosi. She essentially gave him the job, pushing aside the previous top Democrat on the committee, the well-liked and respected Edolphus Towns. Cummings was by far the more confrontational and acerbic of the two, which surely came in handy, because for the Democrats assigned to the Oversight Committee, defending Obama was job one.

We may have had our political disagreements, then as now, but I am troubled that it overshadowed the fact that whether the latest scandal is the shocking treatment of veterans at VA hospitals, improper targeting of conservative groups by IRS officials, or reckless law enforcement operations such as Fast and Furious, there are deep, systemic problems in government. They can be solved only by significant, long-lasting institutional changes, including stronger protections for whistle-blowers, robust congressional investment in oversight, and real autonomy for the independent inspectors general that investigate each executive-branch agency.

These reforms can be aided substantially by making more information on government's actions available to the public through greater data transparency and other open government reforms. More on that later.

As proud as I am of all the work I've done in the private sector, I've come to realize that altering the federal bureaucracy for the better is an even more monumental task in some ways than creating a successful business.

The inventor and businessman Elon Musk is rightly praised for creating Tesla Motors, which may finally make electric cars profitable (even after electric cars floundered for so long that conspiracy theories suggested the government and automobile industry would never allow them to thrive). It's worth noting that he is making his patents available at no cost to anyone who produces pure electric cars, a generous and clever idea to grow a market in which he believes consumers will freely choose his product above all others.

He may have accomplished even more with his SpaceX program. He saw the prices of government-run space launches continually rising and knew there had to be a better way. There are always more efficient means of doing things, but government isn't likely to find them. The offer of a big prize on the open market can work wonders that Capitol Hill committee meetings cannot, including, in the case of SpaceX, designs that will be utilized in Mars missions and cargo shipments to the International Space Station—saving the government billions of dollars in reduced launch costs.

Musk didn't just solve practical engineering problems, though. He sent a message about the power of market incentives to outdo government's bureaucratic incentives. He *showed*, rather than just argued, where NASA falls short. To people willing to think through the implications, he raised the possibility that government might well be spending twice as much as necessary on everything it does. He thereby provided one small course correction to the ship of state the likes of which should be far more numerous and far more routine.

Competition, like protections for whistle-blowers, fosters transparency and shows us both errors and successes we might otherwise have overlooked. And transparency, like oversight inquiries, encourages accountability. Even President Obama turned to the private sector—in the form of the computer experts who had run the extraordinarily efficient technology of his presidential campaigns—to salvage the rollout of HealthCare.gov.

The difficult thing about applying similar incentives to Congress is that it is rare for any one individual to be held accountable for wrongdoing. Voters have recently taken broad swipes at the party (or president) currently in charge, costing the Republicans control of Congress in 2006 as the Iraq War dragged on and costing the Democrats seats in both houses of Congress and control of the House in 2010 and the Senate in 2014 due to dissatisfaction with Obama. Most likely, they will keep periodically punishing whichever party is in charge, which does some good—but human beings are more likely to improve their performance in an atmosphere of individual accountability.

Add to that problem the fact that as the bureaucracy of the executive branch expands, more and more of the government is beyond the direct reach of the voters. Americans will never go to the voting booth to decide the fate of wasteful midlevel Department of Energy supervisors or send a corrupt IRS official packing. Even the broom of democracy can't quite reach some bureaucratic cobwebs.

CHAPTER FOUR

A Life before Government

I was born in Cleveland, Ohio, the second of six children—three boys followed by three girls. My mother, Martha, is Mormon and my father, William, Eastern Orthodox, his parents having immigrated from Lebanon. As a boy, I was baptized in the St. George Antiochian Orthodox Christian Church of my father's faith, attended services with my Mormon mother—and grew up in a predominantly Jewish neighborhood.

It was a nice, truly American combination, and one that would provide greater insight into future world events than I suspected as a child.

I would grow up to travel the world for business purposes, testify before Congress in favor of the North American Free Trade Agreement, and become one of the few Arab-American members of Congress. Whether in commerce, tradition, or law, seemingly small, local differences can have ripple effects on far-distant parts of the system.

Like many sons, I saw my father as not just larger than life but physically large as well. Knowing that he and I are the same height— six feet tall—does not change the strong, impressive way I remember him. Even sticking out his hand and introducing himself—"*Bill Issa*"—carried with it the drive and pride of the self-made man.

Though he was "Will" to my mother and "Dad" or "Daddy" to my siblings and me, he was the same diligent and reliable man to everyone who met him. I can't remember a day he wasn't holding down two jobs (and sometimes three or more), and even when I later spent eighty or a hundred hours a week on my own business, I didn't work any harder than he had.

When my siblings and I were very young, we lived in rented, inexpensive postwar "veterans' housing." In Euclid, Ohio, in 1960, the year I turned seven, we moved into the first house my parents ever bought, which had no basement and was about a thousand square feet, with two bedrooms and a single bathroom. Even counting the back porch, the whole place was probably only about 1,200 square feet. We three boys lived in the small attic upstairs, with few electrical outlets and a single light.

In 1963, my family upgraded slightly to a Cleveland Heights home with an enclosed back porch that my father used as a changing room, since the closets in the main rooms were so small. My sisters were now relegated to the attic, my older brother got his own room, and my younger brother and I shared a room. Officially, it was a three-bedroom house, but with that attic—and at last a basement with a natural-gas furnace—the eight of us fit in quite well.

Now there was room for Dad's nails in mason jars down in the basement, and an unused coal bin in which to store the Christmas ornaments when they weren't in use. That was spacious living! In time we rolled out a rug on the basement floor to create a play area and added a couple needed tubes to a discarded black-and-white TV for further entertainment. You might say that was my first brush with consumer electronics upgrades—a hint of business dealings to come.

For now, though, my entrepreneurial exploits were more humble: as I went into sixth grade and my older brother into eighth, we both secured paper routes. My brother's route was with the *Cleveland Plain Dealer*, which is still in business, and mine with the *Cleveland Press*, which isn't.

I also got a job with the weekly Sun Newspapers owned by Howard Metzenbaum, later a US senator. They delivered to every address in the neighborhood for free, thanks to ample advertising inserts. Customers could place ads of their own, discounted, using a little submission slip they received from time to time with their papers and an invitation to pay to advertise—half to the Sun, half to the paperboy. That was nice for me and for any neighbors wanting to spread the word about rummage sales, because at that time, Cleveland Heights prohibited the display of yard signs for garage sales and even the sale of homes.

As a family with six kids, we had fit in pretty well back in Euclid among big families that were mostly Italian and Irish and usually Catholic. Cleveland Heights, though, was middle class and predominantly Jewish and more successful, well enough off to have maids come in once a week.

That provided my next business opportunity. I started it one weekend with the family's push mower, mowing a whole series of neighbors' lawns. As I picked up the princely sum of a dollar or two per lawn, I was soon able to buy a gas-powered mower I'd seen in a Sun newspaper ad. I tried to duplicate that success by buying a snowblower, but it never gave me quite the same leap in efficiency the gas mower had. I still ended up doing a great deal of shoveling. Lesson learned: some devices provide greater advantages than others. Still, both the mowing and snow removal earned some needed money.

Some of my friends in high school had glimpses of commerce as well. My friend Joel Davis's family owned a chain of bakeries, and he'd remain prominent in the community. Culture matters, too, though, and being immersed in a Jewish community meant I was in a Boy Scout troop that held regular Jewish services on Saturday, coinciding with our regularly scheduled weekend camping activities.

Dad was almost always working, but that afforded me time to get to know some of the other fathers and work as a counselor at a Boy Scout camp called Beaumont and later at a YMCA camp called Centerville Mills, the latter paid for by reselling tubes of chocolate-covered thin mints—several hundred tubes if you hoped to pay for summer camp. But it could be done, if you knocked on enough doors and looked needy enough. The communal camp dining halls, with their socializing and sing-alongs, provided what were probably the joyous times of many a childhood.

Let me offer a few words about Cleveland—an indispensable part of my childhood, my later life, and many of its happy moments.

To many, Cleveland has a less-than-stellar reputation, conjuring up images of smokestacks, urban decay, and grim, gray skies. Perhaps that is understandable. But to those of us who were born there or lived there, that disdain only binds us together. The more one criticizes Cleveland, the more locals will embrace the city and its special standing.

And it *is* special. I've been asked many times if, when I was young, I dreamed of growing up, getting out of my family's crowded houses and moving on from life in the Rust Belt, the bitter winters, the spontaneous combustion of the Ohio River, even the perennial losing ways of Indians baseball in "The Mistake by the Lake" and our beloved Browns and the utter heartbreak of "Red Right 88" (look it up).

Didn't I want to run away from all that?

Are you kidding? To my friends and me, Cleveland wasn't just home, it was *big*. It had everything. It was famous, it was rolling, and heck, we thought it even seemed green. Cleveland rocked. Still does, although I'm not sure I fully recognize today's gleaming downtown that I'm looking forward to returning to in 2016, when Cleveland hosts the Republican National Convention. It will be a party worthy of a legendary city, its great people, and a part of America that deserves an embrace.

That's something else many don't understand about Cleveland. Although we were unfamiliar with the term "diversity" growing up, the city was a quintessential melting pot, and we couldn't have been more comfortable in it. We might have been from different ethnic backgrounds, but we felt as though we had far more in common than not.

For example, being in a Jewish community meant getting to watch many of my peers sweat their way through their bar mitzvah speeches as they entered manhood, then go on to study at Hebrew academies. I was impressed. By contrast, I'd never been a particularly engaged student; I was somehow interested in every activity except the ones school was offering. I studied just enough to get by.

I did, though, apply myself in audio-visual in junior high and high school—setting up TVs and projectors to show the class things such as Walter Cronkite's broadcasts. A little fiddling was always required back in those days to keep the frames from slipping out of alignment. By the time I left high school, Sony's early-model black-and-white video recorders were appearing, but it was another reminder that technology can be two steps forward, one step back:

you never got quite as satisfying an experience from the small TV screens of the day as from a big screen with a film projector.

High school meant an increased interest in both extracurricular activities and girls, and that logically led to being in the stage crew for theater and musical productions. The stage crew itself had few females, but it provided a great opportunity to meet girls without having to have the discipline to learn lines or try out for a part. Many skills I learned there I continued to use throughout life, including painting and woodworking. However, getting a pass out of classes—or sometimes just cutting—to do the work might have done me more harm than good.

For me and for so many other teenagers in America, though, real freedom came to be associated in my mind with driving a car—and not driving with my father.

Though our family at times had more than one car, for years there was only one driver: Dad. My mother, meanwhile, tried to learn to drive for nearly a decade. We would go out on Sundays, usually Dad's only day off, with Mom behind the wheel and Dad doing a perfectly awful job of teaching her. Every six months, she would get a new learner's permit, and we would drive country roads as my father endlessly intoned that she was over the center line, too close to the side of the road, or weaving between the two. My mother never seemed too comfortable with the idea that she was a more than adequate driver and would never flourish behind the wheel until she had the chance to drive *without* my father in the car.

That went on from about the time I was eight years old until my sixteenth birthday—by which time I had paid for driver training using the paper route money and finally got my own license. The very week I got it, Mom asked me to take her out driving instead of Dad. Since I didn't have the kind of driving instructor standing she perceived my father to have, she wasn't as nervous with me advising her, and the lessons went very smoothly.

I just recited what I'd heard for six weeks of my own driver's education classes—including some slick maneuvers that made one far more likely to pass the Ohio driver's test, with its very specific requirements regarding parallel parking and other moves.

Within a few weeks, Mom took her exam and passed the test, which seemed worth celebrating, but it carried a serious downside: I lost the car I would have otherwise been able to use myself if we hadn't had another new driver in the family. To this day, my mother still gives me credit for her getting her driver's license, though she could easily have taken classes on her own.

Family life involves constant negotiations about who has authority over what. Being the middle brother of three, I was also the second oldest of all six kids in the family. That meant my little brother, Ricky, was always ratting me out for bringing candy to bed at night (and not sharing) or other offenses. But there was always that older brother, the one kid in the family who knew, for a time, what it was like to be an only child, even if for only two years.

When my older brother got his license, my father bought the biggest, blackest Ford 500 powered by an imposing V-8 engine that got—maybe—five miles to the gallon around town. It was a four-door sedan unlike anything around today, with a huge trunk that made it a great car for traveling salesmen. The springs in the back had already begun to sag, and it was anything but a cool car by a sixteen-year-old's standards. Still, my brother immediately became the man about town chosen to carry around several, sometimes ten, of his young companions. Unfortunately, that also introduced new temptations to misbehave, sometimes by siphoning gas out of Dad's car—once even leading to Dad running out of gas a short distance from home and becoming very suspicious about it. The gas-stealing habit also provided my brother with enough fuel to pretty well run the old Ford into the ground by the time I got my license, so that car wasn't available to me either.

My brother also had the unfortunate experience of damaging my father's Buick Electra 225 after dropping his prom date back home. He managed to bend all four rims as well as the frame of the car and flatten two tires without actually denting the body. None of us was ever allowed to borrow my father's car again.

Once I got my license, though, my entrepreneurial tendencies kicked in once more. Motivated by a laserlike focus on getting a car of my own, instead of going into low-paid or unpaid jobs such as camp counseling, I drove for a kosher poultry delivery service.

I got the gig thanks to a recommendation from my Boy Scout friend Harvey Fierman to Rabbi Kazen, who was the boss of the business. Rabbi Kazen was a Holocaust survivor and truly devout Orthodox Jew who constantly tried to teach me bits of Hebrew and offered me food or drink or anything else so I would pray with him for a few minutes. I never met a more decent man who suffered more, yet remained true to the fundamental tenets of his faith.

Harvey honestly vouched for my talents but fibbed that I was Jewish on my mother's side. The job paid well, and the tips were even better. Each day, I had to pick up a load of fresh chickens, ducks, and occasionally turkeys. The meat was fresh, but the same could not be said for the station wagons we used for the deliveries, which were old and soaked in leaked chicken blood. You always had to have the windows open.

Despite the smell, that job fed my love of cars. I'd share that with a close friend since junior high, bookworm and future attorney Ben Hunsinger, who had a hard-working German dad and Italian

Catholic mom as well as four siblings and did a stint in the army, making his youth a little bit like my own. Unlike my mom, though, Ben's mother had a driver's license and would pile her own kids and others into their family station wagon and take them camping or on other excursions.

I should add that Ben's mother, Lucille, was much more than just our chauffeur. In fact, she was my first political debating partner, and she was as tough and tenacious a Democrat as any I've tangled with in Congress. We spent hours and hours (over many years) drinking coffee at her kitchen table and going back and forth. I was a Nixon supporter, while she was totally against him. And it just carried forth from there. We were extremely close, and it was an early education that people can disagree without being disagreeable.

Ben got his license a crucial six months before I did—and his grandfather gave him an aging jeep, with front and back seats and a large storage area in the back near the tailgate, perfect for camping. Ben and I were allowed to work on the jeep and paint it even before Ben got his license, and we eagerly did so. Once Ben got his license, we were off. Once I got my license, he let me drive it almost as often as he drove it himself when we were together.

Within a year, though, Ben decided to send that jeep back to his grandparents' farm, swapping it for their old version of a big Checker Marathon, an automobile with the most spacious back seat ever seen in a nonlimousine. Those vehicles had been made and sold all over the country but were almost exclusively used as taxis. A taxi-style car didn't quite suit my teenage needs or budget, though. The answer for me was a 1961 Volkswagen Kombi bus, which was half bus and in the back half pickup. I bought it in exchange for a Schwinn bike, a CB crystal radio (which had only six channels), and $165, still perhaps the most complex purchase of my career.

That VW went everywhere with me, was a hit with kids and counselors at the Centerville camp, and, in keeping with the fashions of the day, was eventually painted on all sides with hippie symbols including the peace sign, which might surprise some of my more liberal critics. It looked exactly like the hippie bus that it wasn't. It survived trips as far as Massachusetts and back on recapped tires that would likely not have survived traveling much faster than fifty-five miles per hour. Downhill, it might make it as fast as sixty-two, but it had to stick to the slow lane and second gear going uphill.

Still, it was a taste of ownership and a feeling of freedom.

High school came to an early end. I liked my car, my jobs, my stage crew time, and other extracurricular activities, but not so much my studies. So in 1970, shortly after my last summer at camp and just a few months after the death of my father's only brother, for whom I was named, I decided to enlist in the army. The Vietnam War was raging, Nixon was president, four students had just been killed at Kent State University, and being drafted was common. Enlistees were rare, so with a mother's signature, it was easy enough to be accepted into the army. Today's recruitment standards are far higher.

Just days after my seventeenth birthday I took my first plane ride in a Piedmont Air prop job taking off from Cleveland and, after a couple stops, landing in Louisville, Kentucky. From there we boarded buses and went to Fort Knox for eight weeks of basic training. I have never been so cold so often as I was in the flimsy cotton uniform and leather boots I was issued, marching up and down the hills, lying on the ground for rifle training, and standing midnight guard duty—well inside a section of the base made up of empty warehouses. We were most certainly not keeping watch over the nation's gold reserves.

Those frigid nights and the tone of basic training convinced me that I had made a big mistake and I needed to be back in high school, preparing for college, getting an education, and never going back to shivering guard duty. Within weeks of starting basic training, I took the GED (general equivalency diploma) exam, passed it, and went on to take additional CLEP (College-Level Equivalency Program) tests. By the end of basic training, by army standards, I had a high school diploma and had completed nearly a year of college.

About halfway through basic training, after taking a battery of exams that were supposed to measure IQ, I was part of a small group of soldiers who were shown a movie about World War II demolition workers who disarmed bombs and mines. It was all very exciting, and despite our sleep deprivation, we stayed until the end, at which point an officer and a senior NCO got up and made the pitch: there were special units called EOD (explosive ordnance disposal) or bomb squads that you could enter only by volunteering. If you did, you left the other forms of training you were undergoing, but you got an exciting opportunity to become an expert in chemical, biological, nuclear, and conventional weapons—and $55 a month additional "hazardous duty" pay.

Readers today will probably scoff at $55 as an incentive to put your hands on live munitions hoping they don't go off while you're disarming them. In 1970, though, a private's pay was about $100 a month. An extra $55 was a fortune. You also got a badge and quicker promotions. I jumped at the offer.

Upon completion of basic training, I went home for a week's leave and discovered my brother had taken my pride and joy Volkswagen to a concert with a group of his friends and driven off-road through the woods to avoid a traffic jam. Pieces of trees were embedded in the bottom of my beautiful vehicle's engine. The fan belt had popped off at some point. He'd still managed to drive it home and park it. But when I started it up, it made terrible sounds that told me the end had already come. With little time and no ability to get it to the next military duty station, I took the beloved vehicle to the junkyard, never to enjoy the many trips I had yet imagined for her.

The early months of 1971 were nonetheless an exciting time as I moved on from basic training to my first duty station, Fort McClellan, near Anniston, Alabama. It was a small base but home of the chemical corps trained to deal with our stockpiles of nerve agent, blood agent, tear gas, and potential biological weapons. We would now learn all about those deadly and terrible weapons, including mustard gas. This only added to the horror I felt years later upon learning that Saddam Hussein was using chemical weapons in his war against Iran and Bashar al-Assad was using them against his own people in Syria.

Fort McClellan had another claim to fame. It was the home of the Women's Army Corps (WAC). All women entering the US Army at that time, unless they were doctors or nurses, would be trained there and then deployed—and, though stationed right next to men all over the world, they would answer only to female officers. Sadly, for a girl-crazy seventeen-year-old, there were absolutely no opportunities to mix chemical training and romantic chemistry as the WACs went through their own orientation.

I was later stationed at little-known Indian Head Naval Weapons Station in Maryland, just outside Washington, DC. There, for decades, every person who trained for EOD, regardless of which military branch they were in, trained together, disarming weapons both conventional and clandestine.

There, great things began happening for me. First of all, I was now only about six hours of hitchhiking away from Cleveland

and could get home on weekends, although I rarely did. That was because with about ten hours of hitchhiking I could instead reach Kent State University. To the world, it was now infamous as the site of the shooting deaths of two student protesters and two student bystanders during antiwar demonstrations. To me, though, it was now the home of a coed who had had my attention for a long time: my girlfriend Pam. It took me as long to make the trip there as I had time to spend with her once I arrived, before heading back to base again.

Another unique thing about Indian Head was that the navy allowed us to have cars—like the gorgeous but malfunctioning 1963 Triumph TR3 that a fellow EOD trainee had to leave behind when he was shipped out. I bought it for $250, in part using the first loan I'd ever taken out in my life, from the Pentagon credit union. Paying it back at $25 a month was tricky, and the car wasn't operational at first, but it was the best-looking car of its day.

Working on that car took up plenty of my spare time, but finally I got it working and was able to drive the car all the way to Cleveland before transferring to my next duty station.

My original ambition to go to Vietnam and really see war was perhaps an aspiration I was fortunate not to realize. Like my father, who served during both World War II and the Korean War, I always seemed to find myself right on the verge of being ordered to a theater of conflict and then ending up in other places.

I was first sent to the 145th EOD Unit in a little place called Manor, Pennsylvania, about an hour from the Ohio border along the Pennsylvania Turnpike. Our job, with no major military installation in the area, was to help both military and civilians with whatever explosive challenges they faced. Often we'd get a call from someone who had come across dynamite in a shed or a souvenir hand grenade or other munitions from a previous war, not knowing whether they were active or blanks. We also found ourselves "burning off" ammunition marked for disposal, cooking it inside a bulletproof container.

It wasn't exciting work, but it was an exciting time. It wasn't all good, though.

When my father was still in his forties, he had his first heart attack. Before long, some of my trips back and forth to see Pam were occasionally replaced by trips to Cleveland to see Dad, who was wondering whether he would have to give up at least one of the two jobs he'd held for so many years. I was weighing whether to use a hardship discharge from the military to help with the family. I applied for it despite mixed feelings. The application was accepted, and in February 1972 I was given an honorable discharge. By that time, my father's health seemed to be improving a bit, though that would prove temporary.

In the summer, I applied to Siena Heights College in Adrian, Michigan, and began classes there in the fall, one year of credit already under my belt. That fall brought not only my adjustment to a college run by Dominican nuns but my first meeting with Marcia Marie Enyart, a young studio art student who'd graduated from a Catholic high school in Sharon, Pennsylvania. She was a talented artist and a good student, and she smoked Salem Lights, a brand I had tried once or twice in the army. I bummed one off her when I glimpsed her in her bohemian-looking overalls and struck up a conversation, and that began a courtship that continued throughout that school year.

I secured a two-year ROTC scholarship at a time when the army needed to keep its relatively small crop of volunteers happy. The condition of the scholarship was that I attend a college that had ROTC training, though. My preference would have been to do that at the University of Michigan, but I was strongly urged to apply to Kent State due to the army's desire to keep its ROTC program alive there after the 1970 shooting deaths of those four students, one of whom had been an ROTC cadet senior.

On the very same day in late September 1973, I began courses at Kent State, fellow transfer Marcia began classes there as well, we eloped to Cleveland to get married—and my older brother, who had been caught stealing cars, was convicted and headed to prison for four years.

The two full years and one term at Kent State went quickly, and I still had to take a couple more business classes to complete my degree, as well as complete flight training paid for by the army. In March 1976, I received my degree from Siena and was commissioned. I was a second lieutenant, armor division (a tank driver), and was promptly shipped off to Fort Knox, Kentucky, that time headed into summer instead of winter and with no guard duty requirement.

As an officer, you're saluted, you outrank every enlisted man and woman in the military, and it's assumed you know a little something on the day you're commissioned. I'd served as an enlisted man, but the hardest challenge as a second lieutenant is realizing how much you still have to learn. Much of the training you get as an armor officer is the same as what your crew receives: maintaining the tank's tracks, maintaining the engine, loading the gun tube, sighting and firing the gun, and maneuvering in order to keep from being targeted by others' weapons. All of that was easy compared to college—and gentlemanly compared to the treatment of enlisted men.

I did face one last serious challenge in the classroom, however: a written exam during which several of us noticed a fellow lieutenant cheating by looking at other people's tests. One of the more senior members of my class eventually turned him in, and we were all required to report what we had seen. That was a good lesson in shared responsibility and holding everyone to the same high standard.

Even though the cheating student looked as thought he might have made a good halfback for the football team, the military was even hungrier for officers, and he was soon discharged. I was selected from among the top of my class to go on to advanced training for battalion support vehicle maintenance at Fort Riley, Kansas, where I was assigned to the Second Regiment of the 63rd Armored Infantry Battalion.

Marcia, meanwhile, had gone from being a bohemian artist to being a fellow ROTC cadet and scholarship recipient and was now also a second lieutenant, specializing in transportation and stationed at Fort Eustis, Virginia. At the end of her training and my training, we arrived together at Fort Riley. But we had drifted apart. When she said she didn't want to be married anymore, I was beyond distraught. You never know in advance exactly how you'll react to something, but once I realized there were going to be two Lieutenant Issas on one base and they were not going to be married, I realized I needed to transfer out of there.

I was able to secure transfer to a little-known unit in California called the Army Combat Developments Experimentation Command. I loaded up my car with everything I had and headed off to a new assignment that would not have happened if not for our separation.

It may seem difficult to believe, but in the mid-1970s, many of our soldiers found themselves on food stamps. Weapons systems were getting old quickly. Maintenance was poor. Facilities were run down. The Jimmy Carter years were very tough on morale and recruiting. I was almost unaware of the problem while at Combat

Developments, though, since it was the site of some of the military's latest, cutting-edge computer hardware, aimed at coming up with new fighting techniques through experimentation, to increase the odds of winning real battles. We were generally able to get the parts and equipment we needed, even purchasing items such as lasers and radio frequency devices from outside the military if necessary. We even had then-high-speed 2400-baud synchronous modems on dedicated lines. That was an early glimpse of the future of warfare.

Those were good years. I was able to advance through the ranks, work with some of the finest officers imaginable, develop leadership skills, and, crucially, learn a lot about the electronics industry that I would enter when I left the army. And it was a time when I was starting to think about what would come next. It helped that the literal girl next door in Monterey, California, where I sometimes stayed for gatherings of officers, was Kathy Stanton, whom I met in 1979 and who early the next year would become—and remains—my second wife.

In the summer of 1978, almost seven years after his first heart attack, my father had a stroke. I was called in by radio from a training area out on Fort Hunter Liggett in southern Monterey County, and a jeep was sent for me. The army's systems for sending me home went into overdrive, and a helicopter flew me the seventy-six miles to the airport in Monterey. There, with some help from the Red Cross, a ticket was already waiting, and I boarded a United Airlines jet for Chicago. I changed into civilian clothes onboard, and then flew to Cleveland.

Because of the military's help, I got to see my father—though just barely. He died early the next morning. He accomplished much and left behind even more, but the burden of the work he shouldered no doubt shortened his good life. He was only fifty years old.

My mother had recently received her nursing certificate and was able to find a job. Most of my siblings were out of the house. There was some insurance money to help my mother pay off the house. By the time my father passed away, he had formed a small business servicing large long-haul trucks and had several employees. I went home many times over the next several weeks to help wind down the business, sell off equipment, find jobs for key employees, and do my best to put things into order.

One seemingly small thing remained: a piece of land that my father had inherited, like his father before him and his father's father before him, in Lebanon. It was not a large tract owned outright but a portion of land shared with other relatives and neighbors. Selling those little pieces of land would be complex, but my grandfather, shortly before his death, had sold a piece of the land there for $10,000. My father had gone there in the mid-1970s and determined, with the help of his cousins, that a portion of the land might be worth over $100,000 if you could find a buyer. In late 1978 and early 1979, I made trips to Lebanon to seek buyers and transfer the property. The country was still suffering from the effects of civil war, and it would remain occupied well into my time as a member of Congress decades later.

That was a blessing because it gave me something to focus on amid the mourning—and because it was the thing that first caused me to visit Lebanon. I got to know my grandfather's brother and sisters while they were still alive. Lebanon had been in a civil war that had lasted a decade, then been occupied by multiple groups: Syrians, Israelis, and a powerful Shia militia—not then called Hezbollah—along with Sunni and Christian militias, remnants of the war, each with its own army. When I visited, it was still necessary to go through multiple checkpoints, some controlled by the Syrians and some by the Israelis, to get to the little town in northern Lebanon that my grandfather had emigrated from in the early twentieth century, when the Ottomans still ruled the area.

It also gave me the opportunity to see buildings that were centuries old and the place where my grandfather, along with his siblings, had been born in the larger region, not long ago called Transjordan, where early Christianity thrived but that most Christians have since fled. My grandfather's town was poor, though I found it beautiful, yet I understood the impetus for much of the emigration to the United States, Brazil, the Caribbean, and Australia.

The trip did enable me to find a buyer for the property and allow me to disburse money both to my mother and to my father's one remaining sister. More important, it allowed me to see a part of the world that I would revisit time and again in other roles. I was an ordinary person then, and people were comfortable telling me exactly what they thought—about the United States, about Israel, about the Saudis, about almost anything. It really did allow me to see things in a clear way that can sometimes elude one in a prominent position—even a member of Congress.

After I left the military in 1980, I applied to work at many large companies—Procter & Gamble, Johnson & Johnson, Paine Webber, and many more—hoping to improve upon the meager earnings of my military years. I got several offers, but as I left active duty and headed home, I realized I wanted some challenge other than just fitting into a big corporation. My old friend Ben Hunsinger's father, Miles, needed a new business partner in his small electronics company. The job was for someone to watch the factory, which made small parts for other companies, while he went out and made sales calls. I took over and was the firm's vice president for about five years.

I loaded up the one car we hadn't sold, my wife's 1967 Volkswagen Karmann Ghia with a little over 100,000 miles on it, to head from California to Cleveland for the job, but without Kathy. She was pregnant and had been told that such a long drive in a rattling old car might be bad for the baby. We agreed on a compromise: she'd fly and I'd drive to Denver; we'd stay for a day at her cousin's home and then drive the rest of the way *slowly*—resisting the temptation to take advantage of the region's very high speed limits.

Despite our slow pace, we still got stopped by a police officer, who insisted I'd been going eighty-two, a speed I promise laws of physics did not allow the poor car to even reach. The officer didn't believe me and said, "I know about them sports cars." At the next exit, I paid the heavy and unjust fine in cash. Two days later and $75 poorer, we arrived in Cleveland.

Toward the end of 1980, I started working the sixteen-hour days that would fill the next twenty years of my life. I would leave before dawn to open the factory before the workers arrived at 6 a.m. and come home well after dark, usually working all or part of Saturday or Sunday as well. But it was always worthwhile. There was always the chance we'd build the next winning product and make a real difference in people's lives.

Those first years during the great economic uncertainty of 1980 and 1981 were the most difficult. At that point, my job was to make products that were usually designed by someone else, with contracts over which we had little control and that could end with only a few hours' notice, all in a labor-intensive process.

We manufactured cables for citizens band (CB) antennas, the coils for electronic bug zappers, and, sometimes, entire products. Sometimes the jobs were menial, such as painting and installing motors, making components for heaters on military jeeps, or producing a printed circuit board that would boost an FM signal for car radios. Each of those products helped prepare me, though, for the production of the products that my company would be best known for in decades to come.

One of our customers, a small company called A.C. Custom Electronics, was making an electronic key code device to prevent a car being started without the owner's authorization. The product wasn't particularly reliable—twist a couple of its wires together and you could make the car start or disable it completely—but it was very profitable, until the owners began squandering the money. This can occur when small businesses experience some early success but get into trouble when ownership starts living beyond its means and engages in increasingly desperate measures to bring in cash to keep it all going. Eventually the bank pulled the plug on A.C. Custom, leaving me with only an IOU for money we'd loaned them to help it through a tough time.

At the time, I did not fully realize the size of the problem I'd gotten into or the ire of many of their customers who had received shoddy goods. Still, I negotiated with the bank to let me buy the molds, the trade name, and the partially assembled inventory of the company. The bank would receive any payments that were still owed the company.

Although the product was soon phased out in favor of ones that worked better, it gave me a start in the industry and a trade name (however tarnished), and I moved forward. Within a year, we were developing a better radio-frequency-based version of the lock, had replaced or repaired nonworking units of the old version that had been shipped to customers, and were building a base of new customers. Things looked good.

Then came the weekend of Labor Day 1982. As Kathy and I and our eighteen-month-old son enjoyed a day at the lakefront and a world-class air show, I had no idea that in a corner of the factory used to construct bug zappers, a piece of test equipment had been accidentally left on; it stayed on all weekend, heating up a wooden table and starting a fire.

At about 2 a.m., after my pleasant day at the lake, a fire department dispatcher called and told me, "There's an active fire in your building." I drove over to find firemen and my business partner, Miles, already on the scene. When it was over, very little of the factory had been destroyed by fire, but the effects of smoldering plastic and scattered paper were everywhere. A thick layer of black soot covered everything but the undersides of tables. The partially plastic residue was nearly impossible to remove. Everything had to be thrown away or painted over.

The damage caused by the well-intentioned firemen was even worse, since the fire took thousands of gallons of water to extinguish, which poured onto cardboard boxes and electronics. Then the rain came. It seemed to rain longer than anything Noah had experienced. It was also unseasonably cold. Products that had survived the fire quickly mildewed. Tools rusted. Revenue was zero for more than two months.

During that time, we exhausted our funds. Some workers found other jobs and never returned. Other staff were forced to go on unemployment compensation, but several came to work anyway and did what they could to help as we put the operation back together in a temporary building we rented. We couldn't pay them, but they helped us clean up, repaint walls, and sift through the remains of our business as we dealt with the extensive damage. We never forgot their kindness or what it meant to us as we got back on our feet.

As dire as things looked, Miles wouldn't give up, and we began working with new products with some of our customers who'd stayed with us. The fledgling car security line made a comeback, though a couple employees left us after the fire and took components with them, becoming our new competitors.

I could write a whole book full of lessons learned about competitors, employees, keeping company secrets, and the like, but as someone only two years out of the army, I had to learn the hard way. People are unpredictable, especially in a crisis in which they think jumping ship is their only option and that the first ship won't survive to complain (or compete) later.

The two brothers who left the company and set up on their own were never huge successes, but they stayed in business in various forms over the years. Surprisingly, their sister, Ernestine Brown, who was the production manager at my business (and kept our workforce together when we were shuttered after the fire and water damage), stayed with us, chastised her brothers for years for their unscrupulous behavior, and is now happily retired in Tennessee with the money she made working with me. Hats off to people like her.

Although the patents issued to me over the next several years as I traveled between our US and Asian operations were in electronics, two major reasons for the success of the business were the dedicated people I hired and the marketing we did. My top priority from 1982 on, really, was selling people the idea of the company as a whole.

That role began that year with my first consumer electronics show. Such shows had begun a few years earlier in New York City, moving to Chicago and then Las Vegas. Each year that I attended, I would meet people I would never have met otherwise, and we would examine one another's products, creating relationships that in many cases endure to this day. The size of our trade show booths grew over the years, but at that first show in summer 1982 at the McCormick Convention Center in Chicago, I had just a small temporary wall covered with black cloth and posters and a few product samples hung up for display.

For the drive from Cleveland, I had piled it all into a Dodge Omni—a slightly larger version of the Volkswagen Rabbit and no more glamorous, but it had a hatchback that made it useful for carrying many items. It also had a reclining driver's seat in which I fell asleep upon arrival, napping peacefully until the unloading crew, thank goodness, knocked on the window, woke me up, and took my small assortment of representative products into the show to set up. I worked the show until well into the evening, handing out business cards and meeting the first of several thousand important contacts I'd get to know over the next few years as Directed Electronics' CEO.

In the meantime, the mid-1980s were a fast-paced time of ever-growing business, new hires, new products, and flights to Asia and elsewhere to locate less expensive or harder-to-find components. Though my business with Miles had recovered, I was less interested in assembling things for others now that I was starting to market my own products. In 1985, Miles and I reached the most amicable parting any two business partners could, and his son, my old friend, joined his father in my place.

From Miles I received some of the most important lessons I've learned about business, including the fact that if your profit margins are dangerously small, you should focus on that problem before worrying about increasing production and sales. No amount of volume will make up for losing money on each unit produced (as the government ought to learn). When you have a profitable production process, it's time to add business. I also found that there are only small gains to be had from penny-pinching on immediate overhead costs if it doesn't help to streamline the overall production process. I put some effort into installing a timer in place to turn the heat off when no one was around in one factory—but mistiming just how long it would take to get the place heated back up in the morning ended up costing us in decreased worker productivity.

A broader lesson from those days, though, was that you tend to flourish when you are making and selling your own products instead of crafting them for someone else. If you're making someone else's products, you're always at the mercy of their sales schedules. If they're *your* products, you can take surplus units to potential new customers, control your own inventory, and staff in accordance with your own production rhythms.

At the same time, I made extensive use of subcontractors because that enabled me to expand or contract the number of vendors I was using in response to demand but to do so without threatening layoffs of my permanent employees. That built and strengthened a mutual trust between the staff and management. Keeping them employed—and empowering them all the way down to the assembly line to make improvements in the production process—meant an improving, learning business instead of one starting from scratch from one big seasonal order to the next. The flexibility created by owning your products and having the liberty to use subcontractors as needed also enables you to serve the needs of customers more efficiently, to be highly responsive to shifts in the market, instead of just focusing on the relationship with one dominant client.

In the spring of 1985, I stopped in California to visit a potential vendor called Astro-Guard, which then mostly made products for other people, as I had. I was looking for additional manufacturing capacity and they were willing to make products for my company, but their vice president for sales, Ron Flansbaum, had bigger plans. He wanted me to buy out the whole company and replace its CEO, expanding the company's auto security operations. We took the bait, and I headed to California again to work there as vice president of Astro-Guard, anticipating the CEO's departure within about two years.

For ten months, I juggled its operations with running a large portion of Directed Electronics' operations back in Cleveland, but it became increasingly obvious that although the Astro-Guard CEO might not have been ambitious, neither was he eager to give up having and spending a large income. He also tended to believe less in the maintenance of a healthy ongoing profit margin than in the joys of continually borrowing money whenever it was available—a formula popular with many people on Wall Street and in Washington, but one that always made me uncomfortable.

Selling the company would not give him quite as much money as he wanted to have at the time, so we realized that he should keep running his company and I should run mine. In early 1986, Directed Electronics was once more an independent business, but with its headquarters in the small town of San Marcos, California, instead of Cleveland, Ohio.

San Marcos looks a lot different today than it did when we first ventured there—yet the industrial facility we moved into and its surrounding streets are remarkably similar. Those are the manufacturing office parks that commonly house light manufacturing and specialized services often unseen by the larger business world: tool-and-die shops, plastic molding purveyors, even classic car restorers.

Like the businesses themselves, the spaces are neither glamorous nor glossy—they are functional, straightforward, and no nonsense. While ours didn't have stained glass, a waterfall, or even enough parking for our employees, to us it was beautiful. It was hot and dusty, the hours were long, and the surrounding trees were mostly ones we planted, but the business was ours, the employees were our teammates, and we embarked on the adventure of a lifetime.

This was the company I had always dreamed of: disciplined, focused, adaptable to change, and committed to moving quickly. This version of Directed Electronics would make no excuses for not succeeding. Though we pledged to succeed together, I believed completely that if we did not, the blame would be mine alone.

Once established in California, we set about to do two things: employ the sound business principles I had learned from (and been taught by) better minds and create the kind of work atmosphere that would draw the best people for the job. If an applicant happened to have an instinct for sales force marketing despite not having a fancy undergrad or graduate degree, she got the job. If he happened to have a gift for engineering and was self-taught (rather than Ivy League trained), we had to hire him.

Jerry Birchfield was our vice president of engineering, and he came to us from Astro-Guard. I was immediately impressed when we first met, as I could see he was not only a gifted engineer, but he was doing it with substandard equipment at Astro-Guard and even using some tools he had bought with his own funds. "Chewing gum and bailing wire" is how he described what he'd had at the former business. We were determined to change that.

Armed with the proper investment in the business, Jerry and his team could take us as far as imagination could go. That was all the more remarkable and admirable because Jerry did not have an engineering degree—or even a college degree. Like me, he'd been in the military and learned some very important things about what to do—but also what *not* to do.

"Starting at Directed had everything—risk, reward, and excitement," he says.

We didn't use the term at the time, but we were building a "culture." Of course, there were hard work and the long hours to go with it, sometimes under hard deadlines and occasionally in a soft market. But the company was possessed of a can-do spirit for which I can't take sole responsibility, although I did my level best to encourage by example.

At the time, the electronics industry could be a very unpredictable—and very unlawful—business environment.

For example, it was a routine practice for our products, once shipped to a port and opened up as part of a cargo container, to be pilfered right from the dock. It was that bad. That necessitated that we change—at some expense—our own cargo containers so that only we would have access to our products.

Sometimes a particularly ambitious salesman would venture overseas, purchase, say, ten thousand units of a product similar to ours, sell them in the United States, pocket the money, and move on to something else. That caused a glut of product and a gap in service, warranty, and reliability.

Also, at any moment, businesses would spring up, order products from us, and sell them for a while to retail customers—then disappear, vanishing with both our product *and* the money owed to us for them. This is not unheard of in practically any sales endeavor, but it was a near-epidemic condition in our industry.

Though I was obviously concerned about being taken advantage of and cared about what we were losing every time a fly-by-night shop shut down, I knew we were also suffering a loss to the standing, reputation, and integrity of all of consumer electronics. And I believed then as now that corruption tolerated in one part of something will erode the good parts in short order. If our business landscape were reduced to a lawless Wild West, there would be no way for us to climb to the top honestly. That was one of the primary reasons I got involved in forming a stronger association of secure systems and, later, working with colleagues in leading the Consumer Electronics Association.

Just as I am convinced that good government can yield good political results, honest business practices are without a doubt the shortest path to durable business success.

Several times, we were presented with a tricky challenge: as we prepared to ship large amounts of product about which we had nagging doubts but with which we had no proven problems, we would make the decision to hold them all back until after we verified our concerns or fixed the defects. That could be expensive, but it was a bargain when it came to one's internal peace of mind and external reputation.

Routinely, our competitors would seem to undercut our price by offering a lower cost to a few customers while overcharging the rest. We maintained a transparent price structure that eschewed side deals and was the same in private as in public.

The point here is not to trumpet my company's virtue but to emphasize that in trying to do the right thing we were rewarded with the confidence of our customers and their help and assistance when we needed it. Cutting corners might have gotten us someplace that looked promising, but it would have been a longer route than the way of the straight line and our name would have been tarnished. As Jerry Birchfield puts it, "The best kind of shortcut is a straight line."

This mind-set certainly came in handy when we were working to innovate and break out from the pack.

One memorable way we did this was through the extensive use of print advertising, trade publications, and even the creation of our own magazines that described in detail the state of the security industry and appealed to the serious business leader. Glenn Busse in particular developed the look and feel of our company's promotional materials. He says, "This was the kind of creativity others weren't doing. We weren't sure it would work, but we believed, and it did."

In today's wired and virtual online marketplace, a print strategy may seem like ancient history. But those trade magazines and print publications were the social media of their day and connected us to more electronics enthusiasts more quickly and in more ways than anything else we could have done.

As we grew, we moved to a larger facility in San Marcos, then to part of and then all of another building, and then another. At every stop, we planted trees (usually palms) as a means of bringing a natural feel to our industrial work. Today, some of those trees are still standing, taller than ever.

Finally, we established our multibuilding campus just down the road in Vista, where Directed Electronics remains today. It is totally unlike the single San Marcos space in which we started, but it carries with it, I think, the same committed principles that honor each aspect of the core relationship of product, vendor, and customer.

Even in the years we were adding more employees and more equipment and doubling the business each year, we worked hard to keep our identity intact. Glenn Busse observes, "Usually, the larger the company, the less communication. But Directed retained a similar feel as a small, midsize, and then very large company." Jerry Birchfield describes it this way: "There was never anybody you couldn't talk to, and vice versa."

One way we tried to foster this openness was what eventually became known as my "walkabouts"—really nothing more than my touring the various stations of the business on foot and at fairly random times. Those were anything but the kinds of spot inspections one experiences in the army; I was only trying to bring the front office to the shipping door, the back area, the testing bench—and even the break room. It was a departure from the kind of "top-down" management style, and I certainly would have appreciated it when I was working closer to the other end.

I'm not a classically trained electrical engineer, but that allowed me to lend some help and perspective to the people who were "on the bench" testing and perfecting our products. I'm not credentialed in "Lean Six Sigma" management techniques, but that opened up and improved our systems because we welcomed any ideas that would create greater efficiency. I don't have an MBA, but that brought me closer to the sales force while we figured out what customers wanted and the best ways to get it to them again and again.

Those walks were not only good for morale (I also made sure to do one every day of my 1998 campaign for US Senate), they also kept us all in touch and in tune with all aspects of the business, some of which were not so easy to see from afar. It also inspired in everyone a willingness to speak up and express what they knew best. I don't believe we used the word "empowerment" in those days, but that's what it was: we invested authority, responsibility, and accountability in *everyone*, and rather than avoid it, our team grabbed it with gusto.

I recommend this approach to anyone in a management position: give employees what they can use and the opportunity to own a piece of the larger project, and far more often than not, you'll be amazed at what they will devote in heart and soul and mind. In the decades we were in business, I saw that at least one time every single day.

There is a photo that sits in my congressional office in Washington, my district office in Vista, and my living room at home. It's a picture of the entire staff of Directed Electronics in the mid-1990s, and it represents exactly the kind of company we wanted to build and wanted to be. It is a collection of people who, if you saw them individually, might not seem as though they have a great deal in common: younger and older, white collar and blue collar, casually dressed and in business attire, twenty-year industry veterans with long careers and new professionals just starting out, from a host of different and diverse backgrounds.

I love that picture because there we all were, huddled and happy, united in what we did every day and utterly together as one group. In his slight north Alabama drawl, Jerry Birchfield called it "a bottom-to-top camaraderie"—richly rewarding in any language.

Meanwhile, Gary Shapiro recruited me to be involved in what would become the Consumer Electronics Association (CEA), and I would participate at various levels from the 1980s until I was sworn into Congress in 2001, eventually rising to become the association's vice chairman and then chairman in 1998.

Those were great years for the industry, with constant change and new products, due largely to the integration of microprocessors into products, giving us the ability to do things of which we'd never before dreamed. Serving on the board allowed me to meet with corporate executives, both young entrepreneurs and presidents of long-established domestic and foreign businesses, such as Microsoft, Sony, Samsung, Sanyo, and Panasonic, whose leaders could be very helpful confidants of and advisers to a small, new company and who understood the bigger picture of the marketplace.

During the 1990s, I became chairman of the Vehicle Security Association as well and merged it into the Car Audio Sound Association and later combined them with the Electronic Industries Association, which had existed since the early days of radio and was pivotal in creating the Chicago and Las Vegas electronics shows. The fusion created the Electronic Industries Alliance (EIA, which disbanded a few years ago, after I had moved on to Congress). Overseeing many of those changes helped put me onto the board of CEA. As I rose to the chairmanship of CEA, a rift grew between it and EIA of a sort common when one group (the budding CEA, in this case) produces a great deal of money and another (EIA) wants to consume it (for trade shows, education, and other purposes).

Needless to say, I would witness conflicts of that sort time and again in the years ahead in Washington. In that case, I eventually helped orchestrate the divestiture of one group from the other. The early stages of coordinating all of that activity also helped bring me to the attention of the Greater San Diego Chamber of Commerce, which would soon lead to me traveling to Washington and getting my first in-person glimpse of Congress, an organization that would prove to have internal tensions of its own.

CHAPTER FIVE

From Business Veteran to Government Rookie

S hortly before the historic November 1993 vote on the North American Free Trade Agreement (NAFTA) with Mexico, the San Diego Chamber of Commerce asked me if I would testify on its behalf before the House Committee on Ways and Means. I spoke mostly about my individual experience and what it revealed about the great importance of free trade across borders. In my case, I didn't import anything from Mexico, but I did do a great deal of exporting to Mexico of my car security system. That business was highly taxed, and under NAFTA the fees would be reduced or eliminated, helping both buyer and seller, one of countless ways that government can help the economy by just getting out of the way.

I felt no special thrill while testifying before Congress. The large, stately, ornate, prestigious Ways and Means room, with its imposing dais, had only a handful of members present, including my congressman (and predecessor), Ron Packard. Ron introduced me to the Democrats presiding over the hearing, including the very senior Representative Sam Gibbons of Florida, as well as a fellow

Californian, Robert Matsui, who could not have been more kind and welcoming. Maybe that helped keep the Democrats from being too rough on me, as they were far less supportive of NAFTA than Republicans.

I read my statement, giving little thought to the fact that I wasn't even wearing a suit—just a sports jacket and gray slacks. I was certainly not imagining that less than a decade later I would become the next person to represent Packard's congressional district.

Most of my time in the 1990s was spent either on supporting my business or on legal work related to patents and trademarks. My company's success depended on protecting itself from look-alikes and knock-offs, such as "Sniper" car alarms imitative of our Viper, which sometimes meant being at odds with others in my industry. I still had an obligation to work with them in good faith within CEA, though.

Just as I could not during this time imagine later serving in the House of Representatives, I did learn quite a bit about members of Congress—both current and former.

Late in my tenure with EIA, we selected a new president to lead the trade association. Dave McCurdy was a Democrat from Oklahoma and a former member of Congress. He headed the House's Permanent Select Committee on Intelligence and was even briefly a presidential candidate in 1992.

Shortly after McCurdy's selection, I received a phone call from House Majority Whip Tom DeLay (R-TX), who was nicknamed "the Hammer." I soon found out why.

He'd been an exterminator in his business life and was proud to say that he maintained his license even as a member of Congress. He strongly urged not hiring McCurdy and said that, as a Democrat, Dave simply wouldn't have the relationships or the influence to effectively help the organization. I heard him out, but I was pretty surprised at what he was saying. Did he think we would change our minds because he told us to?

I told DeLay that he was a public servant and shouldn't be telling any private citizen or association what to do. And that was the end of the conversation.

(When I met Tom later on after first being elected to the House, I was happy that he didn't seem to remember the exchange.)

I did mention the call to other members of the EIA board, though. And while we didn't dump Dave as DeLay had asked, our time together proved neither short nor always sweet.

Here's why: McCurdy came to EIA just as CEA was at the peak of its profits and success and was effectively paying for the rest of the alliance—the building, the employees, and most of their activities. We had tens of millions of dollars in the bank and could have funded EIA on investments alone for years.

Dave may have been out of Congress, but he was still a politician at heart. He recognized that despite the flow of funds, there were more EIA members who were not members of CEA than who were—and that CEA was not an independent corporation despite its importance. He set about very quickly to round up the EIA board member votes needed to declare all of CEA's funds available for EIA to do with as it wished. I saw firsthand why so many people think congressmen can't wait to get their hands on other people's money.

The rest of us, who had poured a great deal of money into the consumer division over the years, objected vehemently. What Dave didn't understand about trade associations—but has probably come to understand running a couple others since that time—is that they are made up of individuals, often from very different backgrounds and even from competing businesses, who come together voluntarily to pursue common interests in an atmosphere of goodwill. Our association's effort to encourage free and fair trade policies was just one example. We also worked together to develop mutually agreeable safety and environmental standards and other consumer-friendly reforms.

Although Dave rounded up a majority vote, he soon discovered that it had little interest in a knock-down fight with a minority with which it wanted to be on good terms. An ugly rift would also likely have meant the collapse of the annual consumer electronics shows and the evaporation of the CEA-produced money if members began exiting.

We had to fix that, so one long weekend, we all met on neutral ground at a hotel adjacent to O'Hare International Airport in Chicago to work out the terms of our relationship and, if necessary, divorce. Industry stalwarts in attendance included Jerry Kalov, who often made a point of saying he was loyal to neither political party (describing himself as a "Democan" or "Republicrat") and who was crucial to the peacemaking in this case. As a past chairman of EIA and someone who'd helped hire McCurdy, he persuaded people that we needed to find a resolution that would keep EIA united and stronger, not divided and weaker.

Jerry, Dave, and my friend Gary Shapiro were really the ones who negotiated the truce: a large sum of money would be transferred to EIA—one that would increase in size if we fled the agreement before seven years elapsed—while CEA and the other divisions of EIA would henceforth simply constitute an alliance of voluntary members.

Gary and I knew that an eventual separation was likely inevitable, but for now the arrangement allowed us to grow and develop our own trade show as a separate corporation and retain nearly half of our cash in return for disbursing the other half to other members; really a sort of advance payment on what we likely would have given them over the next several years anyway.

Within only a few years, EIA disbanded itself, while CEA grew to become the undisputed industry leader and one of the highest-profile technology associations in the country.

Gary has remained a friend during and since that time of transition and is generous in crediting me with helping to forge the agreement under which he continues to be president of the association (recently rebranded the Consumer Technology Association), a role as big and as important as practically any Fortune 500 CEO job. He does this with ease and style, even as he periodically reinvents the organization and its pivotal trade shows to keep them relevant.

Leaving Chicago that day, I recalled that Gary and I had first met in Las Vegas at a CEA trade show. I was setting up my company's exhibit display and politely declined the help of the convention center's union assistance. I wasn't trying to make a statement; I just knew where everything should go and wanted to do it myself. Turning down a Las Vegas labor union and doing the work yourself? That was apparently a sin in that city.

So the union announced that it would picket my exhibit, disrupting some of the more than 60,000 visitors attending the show, or, worse, picket the entrances and affect all of them. If that happened, the show would never get off the ground because the other union workers wouldn't cross the picket lines.

Gary met with the union head and worked out a deal: they could picket when the show ended and in that way preserve their claim of jurisdiction. I thought it was a great idea, and it made me, in Gary's words, the first man he ever met who beat the house in a union dispute in Las Vegas.

Getting a business organized, unified, and running right is precisely the kind of thing I've always enjoyed doing and what I always wanted to do from the time I was a teenager.

I certainly did not expect (or even entertain thoughts of) a life in politics.

Some people decide in their youth that they want to be artists or scholars, work with their hands, or follow where a more random path leads them. Bill Clinton told people when he was a teenager that he would one day run for president and even collected money for a congressional run while still in college.

My experience was different. I was, broadly speaking, civic-minded, interested in Boy Scouts, the YMCA, and military service, but I didn't think much at all about politics. I did pay attention to policy, though, and in the late 1970s, I saw that the choices Jimmy Carter was making were beginning to affect the economy in ways that are difficult to imagine today: double-digit inflation, a prime rate above 10 percent, depressingly high unemployment, and a new word added to our economic vocabulary: stagflation.

Another hallmark of the Carter years that I saw firsthand was a hollowed-out military in which the army couldn't even keep soldiers off food stamps or provide them with repair parts for their vehicles.

It was in that inhospitable environment that I began to look into starting and running a small business. My timing seemed bad, though luckily, times were about to change both politically and economically.

Despite the struggle of running a business in those early years, I assumed it would be the basic destiny of my life, which was fine with me. I felt truly liberated to be making and designing things and was happy to be someone who dreams up new products, has them designed, makes sure they're perfected, gets them sold, and does it over and over and over again.

But when you're signing the fronts of paychecks and paying personal, corporate, and payroll taxes, certain things get your attention.

Ronald Reagan was president during that time; he was emphasizing smaller-government and free-market themes, I was doing well, and my products were selling. That was in no small part because of Reagan's policies, which helped get government out of the way. Inflation was brought under control, the cost of money went down, the economy surged, and people were buying consumer products again.

For our industry, it was certainly true that car security systems sell far better when more people are buying new cars than in times when people are trying to eke a few more years out of their older vehicles.

Having enjoyed the Reagan years, it seemed a simple matter to transfer my hopes to his successor, George H. W. Bush. But his betrayal of his "no new taxes" pledge taught me to be more politically aware. Bush's undoing of Reagan's flatter and fairer 28 percent top tax bracket really got my attention—not by raising the taxes I would have paid in the military or when first starting my company, but by raising the sorts of taxes I was paying by the late 1980s and early '90s, when my company was succeeding, expanding, and creating new jobs.

Although Bush justified the new taxes as a necessary response to recession and deficit, I saw it as a reminder that even under a Republican president, government could grow faster than it needed to and that taxpayers would inevitably be sent the bill. Clearly, if Bush had been willing to fight for the reform of entitlements and other government spending, he might never have felt the need to surrender to the Democrats' demands for higher taxes—and tarnish his credibility as well.

I listened closely to Ross Perot and was briefly convinced that he had some of the right answers. I disagreed with him on some issues but agreed that the real problem was government's unwillingness to rein in its spending, not a resistance on the part of the rich or the middle class to paying their "fair share" (and more).

If I had only known then the amount of government spending that goes to completely wasteful programs or that simply takes from some people and gives to others, I would have been even more furious.

But it got me involved. And the government's economic bungling surely helped sweep Bill Clinton into office two years later, still talking about the "greed" of the 1980s.

But who were the greedy people of the 1980s? He surely meant people like me. But I was someone who had left the army in 1980 driving a Karmann Ghia with nearly 100,000 miles on it, a wife nearly eight months pregnant, and a dream of going into business at a time of recession, unemployment, and high interest rates. I can assure President Clinton that greed was the furthest thing from my mind.

I had enjoyed the Reagan years and the opportunity they gave me to do business at home and around the world. I had succeeded. Our family was secure. Now the president of the United States was denouncing people like me.

Californians, for better or worse, tend to think they can change the world, so when Clinton became president, I became a major donor to the Republican Party, seeking out Republican National Committee chair Haley Barbour and within a short time contributing $100,000. It made me a "Team 100" member, with access to many House and Senate leaders, all of whom were happy I was giving and, as politicians will do, told me how interested they were in my ideas and opinions. It took me only a short time, however, to realize that most of them were interested only in my checkbook.

In 1993, I began to consider taking a more direct hand in political decision making and took a brief look at the idea of running for a San Diego–area seat in the House of Representatives occupied by a political newcomer and Democrat named Lynn Schenk. She had been a Washington lawyer and in her brief stint in Congress had voted in favor of the largest tax increase in US history and against NAFTA, the sort of antibusiness moves by government I was growing to dislike and ones that put her noticeably at odds with her trade-dependent district within San Diego. One of the largest employers there, contributing to its prosperity, was a semiconductor and telecommunications company called Qualcomm, the sort of business that would be hard hit by the policies she endorsed.

More than a dozen candidates had run for that seat in the 1992 primaries and election, but they all now seemed to be exhausted. That gave me a chance to run, and for a seat that was not obviously safe for the very new incumbent. My wife, Kathy, who is certainly smarter than I am, asked me a simple question: Are you the best qualified, the one most likely to win this election? You'll have a teenager at home, she reminded me, and a business growing by leaps and bounds that you work at day and night. Are you really the person who should be running?

That led to a poll of potential voters, and I quickly changed my mind as I realized that there were three potential candidates better positioned to be the Republican challenger: Superior Court Judge Dick Murphy and San Diego County Supervisors Ron Roberts and

Brian Bilbray. Although the numbers were fairly close, Murphy appeared to be the best known of the three, Bilbray the least. As I approached each of them, though, I found that Dick Murphy didn't want to give up his judge's pension, for which he still had to work a few more years, and Roberts didn't think he represented enough of the district. Bilbray was more eager. He was young, handsome, and blue collar, and had come up through the ranks with a good reputation. He is also a dedicated public person and genuinely cares about doing the right thing. He seemed quite electable.

Bilbray's staff director at the time, John Woodard, was constantly strategizing, selecting people for Brian to meet, and doing much of the daily organizing. I showed both of them the numbers suggesting that Brian was far more electable than I was. Both were a bit wary of giving up their current jobs, which left them time to surf the Pacific Ocean as well. Within a few days, though, they told me they were in.

In 1994, Brian was a good candidate in a good year. Woodard brought in a score of good people to help with both fund-raising and management. Brian was elected, and I felt empowered, a part of history. Having done little more than take a poll and deliver it to an appropriate candidate, I was nonetheless convinced that politics would be part of my future.

More than two decades earlier, San Diego had suffered a far more embarrassing political year. In 1972, the Republican National Convention was to take place in the city but was pulled just three months prior to the event due to serious organizational problems, even after plenty of commemorative T-shirts and souvenir items had been produced. Some San Diego Republicans were determined to make up for it by bringing the 1996 convention to the city. Gerry Parsky, who chaired San Diego's convention effort, summoned me to a strategy meeting featuring other local party stalwarts including Alex Spanos (the owner of the San Diego Chargers) and Steve Cushman (the owner of one of the area's largest car dealerships). We lobbied successfully to win the convention.

Over the next eighteen months, we met regularly and broke down how we'd run the event in a manageable way. Steve Cushman would handle logistics. I would coordinate some ten thousand volunteers, about seven thousand of whom ended up being involved on convention days.

After the success of the convention, my sights were set on the seat held by Senator Barbara Boxer (D-CA). In 1998, many believed Boxer was beatable. I had by then been San Diego's Entrepreneur of the Year, made *Inc.* magazine's list of the 500 fastest-growing companies in America not once but twice, and had a highly profitable company that paid its workers well and never had a single layoff all the time we were in California. It seemed like the perfect story, and it might have been if I'd had the chance to tell it.

Early in the campaign, things seemed to go well, and I was able to travel the state and make media appearances. At least some people now knew who Darrell Issa was. However, I soon found myself up against opposition research from both my Republican primary opponent, Matt Fong (then the state treasurer), and Barbara Boxer's Democratic machine.

The first blow came from the *Los Angeles Times*. A reporter who specialized in sneak attacks, half-truths, and outright lies, Eric Lichtblau, pored over my past and interviewed numerous people I had worked with or known over the preceding decades, printing only the tiny handful of the worst-sounding recollections he found. He interviewed the two brothers who had ditched my company but not their sister, who had stuck by me and volunteered to be interviewed. A few weeks before election day, his article came out, accusing me of everything from arson and car theft to business fraud and threatening someone with a gun. It was a hodgepodge of false accusations, but it shifted the momentum of the race in favor of my opponent, whose campaign had been faltering.

In the waning days of the campaign, an article also came out in the *San Francisco Chronicle* attacking the whole premise that I was an army veteran in good standing. It didn't do so by attacking my time as a lieutenant but rather by repeating a series of accusations from my days as a private, including the assertion by a staff sergeant that when I was seventeen, nearly three decades before the Senate race, I had been a bad soldier and had even stolen his car at one point, which is not true.

As a young private, it is true that I was more interested in hitchhiking to see my girlfriend at Kent State than being a model soldier, and my father's illness also tugged at my loyalties more than did the military. I had enlisted at seventeen and was not yet eighteen when my father had his first heart attack—but I then set my sights on becoming an officer, going on to be a lieutenant and then captain.

Still, the story was an ambush, the worst kind of last-minute smear. My press team was livid. At the time, most papers wouldn't print that kind of piece this close to an election, when a candidate had little or no time to respond. We protested loudly, appealing all the way to the newspaper's editor (the actress Sharon Stone's then-husband, Phil Bronstein), who listened politely and stuck with the piece. It fit well into an overall narrative of Issa as a fellow with a checkered past.

I narrowly lost the Republican nomination to Fong. If I hadn't, I no doubt would have wasted much of my time during the general election fighting the same accusations instead of debating Boxer.

I have no regrets for that loss, but only because of what happened afterward: Fong went on to raise millions of dollars and still be soundly defeated. If he, the state treasurer, lost by 10 points, a virtual unknown like me, facing vicious attacks, would surely have met a similar fate. That doesn't change the fact that it hurt. Up until that time, I had enjoyed a positive perception in my community and business circles, and even though friends and neighbors politely responded to the articles by saying "That's just politics," they still must have read the articles and wondered.

The *Times* article was especially disappointing. I had made a loan to A.C. Custom Electronics, which was owned by two brothers (Gary and Joey Adkins) and another man. They deceived me, telling me that the money would be used to pay off a bank loan. None of it was. The bank was in the process of collecting all their receivables and repossessing all their assets. The only thing I had was ninety percent of the stock in a now-dead company, so the bank agreed to let me buy the leftover tools and spare parts, which wasn't much.

Gary and Joey Adkins didn't care for the fact that I called the bank. They're lucky I didn't call the cops.

The *Times'* report made it seem like a ruthless maneuver—but all I did was step in to recover what they'd stolen from me and then try to save the business. Had the reporters bothered to ask Gary and Joey Adkins' sister, Ernestine, her daughter, or the rest of the company's workforce, they might have learned that those people didn't walk to work with us—they ran. By stepping in, we saved their jobs and also saved face with the customers who had given up on them.

Similarly, when my employees and I had managed to clean up and revive our factory after the 1982 fire, I regarded it as a great achievement, but the *Times* dug up initial unsubstantiated arson allegations by the insurance company, which was keen to avoid paying us even a tiny amount. Ultimately, the company paid the insurance claims, even if we didn't receive as much as I had hoped and only a portion of our real damages. Such things play a role in my sometimes looking at my record as one of great success and at other times as one marred by big failures. But in politics, either you move on or you quit.

In an odd bit of compensation, I won a patent lawsuit against our chief business competitor at the same time I was losing the 1998 primary and thus, aside from a huge bill for lawyers, made our company $10 million richer the day after the election, which I announced to my employees, along with my intention to remain at the company. I would have preferred to be vindicated by both the law and the voters, but if I had to choose one on that day, it wouldn't have been a political nomination.

A year later, though, our congressman, Ron Packard, announced he would not run for reelection in 2000. My company was doing well, my son was about to head off to college, and I decided that this smaller race, with a great deal of community support still behind me, was definitely winnable.

Everything went right in my 2000 campaign. My main opponent was actually my state senator, Bill Morrow, who had been elected numerous times and didn't have to give up his seat to run for Congress. He had the fund-raising ability that goes with already being an elected official and had the endorsements of evangelical pastors and mayors, city councilmen, county supervisors, and law enforcement officials. I was undaunted. My name recognition was as high or higher, and the field was crowded. I knew, too, that if I lost this one, I wouldn't run for office again. If I won and served a few years, it would help restore my reputation. Having served four years as an army officer, I was unwilling to let the smears in the press be the final chapter in my public life.

In the Senate race, much of the campaign money had come from my own savings, and that was true of this House race as well. But this time, I called on people I knew throughout the country to give, and they did. Every day in that race, I knew I would have to be actively campaigning and gaining voter support. I also knew that my opponents, particularly Morrow, would use all the material that had been dredged up in the Senate race two years earlier by the *Chronicle* and the *Times.* I was ready.

When Morrow pulled out my military record and tried to contrast my being a "bad" private with his being a marine judge advocate general (JAG) officer, I produced stellar efficiency ratings of my service written by a colonel under whom I'd served and also by a lieutenant colonel named Wesley Clark, both of whom had recommended me for immediate promotion. Morrow was surprised and obviously hadn't considered the fact that the slurs about me in the press were the full story.

Morrow also made the mistake of trying to play the race card. My father's parents were both from Lebanon, my grandfather having emigrated to the United States as a teen and my grandmother as an infant. My surname, Issa, is an Arabic word for Jesus. So when Morrow found that one contributor to my campaign was an individual named Tom Nassif (and who indicated his business as "Gulf States"), he assumed that there was nefarious foreign influence and suggested to the press that I might be tainted by anti-Israeli Arab money. Demonstrating how wrong he was turned out to be fun.

We arranged a press conference with all the major local newspaper reporters and introduced them to Tom—specifically, Ambassador Tom Nassif—who had served in the Reagan administration, first as deputy protocol officer for the White House, later as deputy assistant secretary of state for Near Eastern and South Asian Affairs, and finally as the US ambassador to Morocco.

Morrow is generally a good man, but it had been a while since he had run a serious campaign, and he made mistakes. One of his errors that arose in that same press conference was noting that Kathy and I, normally big Republican donors, had once, in 1992, given $2,000 to a liberal Democrat, Bill Monning, who was seeking to fill the House seat vacated when Leon Panetta exited to become Bill Clinton's director of the Office of Management and Budget.

Democrat Sam Farr easily beat Monning, who was happy to say how thankful he was for that contribution from me and from his cousin Kathy, my wife. Our ties as a family had transcended, however briefly, our vast political differences, he explained.

The press proceeded to have a field day at Morrow's expense, and I won the primary overwhelmingly. I've been elected and reelected a total of eight times. I've had the good fortune to be able to run on my record and trust that most of the voters in my district now know me and discount the worst things said about me in the press.

When I arrived in Congress, having won the primary decisively and the general election by double digits, I was pretty full of myself. I was the outgoing chairman of the Consumer Electronics Association. I knew Bill Gates and other giants of the industry, and they knew me. I thought I should have a committee of comparable importance in government, and I practically demanded to be on the Energy and Commerce Committee.

But in Congress, most everything is determined by seniority. Even the physical Capitol Hill office you occupy during each two-year term is determined by the congressional class with which you arrived and by your ranking, of which I had none. It took me a little while to understand that, and I discovered it the hard way. Though many in the tech community sent in letters suggesting that I be appointed to the Energy and Commerce Committee, no freshmen were being put on what are referred to as the "A" committees.

Luckily, I had a backup plan. Despite not being a lawyer, I hoped to get onto the Judiciary Committee, which among many other matters handles immigration reform, something very important to my district, and patents and copyright law, on which so much of my business had been based. Another nonlawyer and colleague, Sonny Bono, was also interested in an assignment to the committee, in part because of the legal wrangles he'd been through over songs such as "I Got You Babe." With the help of my background in intellectual property disputes, I was assigned to the committee.

The House leadership also accepted my request for appointment to the Committee on Foreign Affairs, which in early 2001 was not regarded as a place of high status. It was a good committee, but those were seemingly quiet times on the foreign affairs front. The committee was seen as having little "juice" and offering little obvious benefit to any member of Congress or constituents not intimately tied to foreign countries. Still, I was happy to get it.

The committee chairman was a giant of a man, in both physical size and political significance. Representative Henry Hyde (R-IL) had just completed his six-year stint as chairman of the Judiciary Committee and was now in his late seventies.

Have no doubt, though, that Henry was in charge. On the opening day of Congress, he was working on naming subcommittees and assigning members with the help of his ranking member, the late representative Tom Lantos (D-CA), a Holocaust survivor from Budapest, Hungary, who was as staunch a liberal as Henry was a conservative.

Traditionally, the subcommittees were defined by region: North America, South America, Asia, Europe, Africa, and the Middle East, and usually an additional Human Rights Subcommittee or the like. As Henry and Tom were finishing, Representative Cynthia McKinney (D-GA) called out, "Mr. Chairman, Mr. Chairman!"

I didn't really know her—or her reputation as an eccentric—at the time. Henry replied, "For what purpose does the gentle lady from Georgia seek recognition?" She launched into a diatribe objecting to Egypt being in the Middle East subcommittee and not the Africa subcommittee. Historically, Egypt has been in the Middle East committee because of its conflict and accords with Israel and with Jordan and other Arab nations. Other Arab countries less involved in those conflicts, such as Algeria, Tunisia, Libya, and Morocco, remained in the African subcommittee. McKinney should have known full well that there was nothing novel about the arrangement.

Yet as she voiced her objection, she said, "If not for the white man at the dais," Egypt would be in the Africa subcommittee. I learned a great deal about Henry's ability to disarm a tense situation with warmth and humor when he responded by pausing and saying "I would assume the gentle lady from Georgia is referring to the chairman's white hair," as he stroked his full, silvery mane and moved on. Lantos, even though from McKinney's own party, then proceeded to explain the inappropriateness of her comment from a civil rights standpoint and as a matter of basic civility.

Henry prioritized carefully, inviting Secretary of State Colin Powell to address us repeatedly about foreign policy and, after the 9/11 attacks, dispatching numerous delegations to other countries to help unite the world with the United States. Even in the months before 9/11, Henry authorized me, a freshman, to lead the first delegation to the new, young president and dictator of Syria, Bashar al-Assad. I had no idea what a great honor it was to be chosen to lead those delegations. He made sure we were accompanied by a Republican and a Democrat staffer, both of whom were highly informed about that region.

As for the region, at that time, there was some optimism that Assad would turn out to be a reformer, rather than an oppressive tyrant like his father. Unfortunately for the Syrian people, he has proven to be more of the same if not worse.

One of Henry's greatest accomplishments may have been when he, Powell, and President George W. Bush shepherded through Congress the landmark African and Caribbean AIDS initiative legislation. It was aimed in part at education, and although AIDS has not been eradicated, the program went a long way toward controlling the disease throughout those regions.

Henry also promoted the Millennium Challenge. For too long, foreign aid had been thought of simply in terms of how much money we doled out and occasionally the additional question of what, if anything, we were getting in return. Aid had often been tied to some other priority. If we needed a military base in some country, we were more likely to give it aid than if we didn't need a base. If we needed a vote in the UN, it might lead to aid. Many of the world's poorest countries received aid in spite of terrible corruption and a complete lack of accountability.

As we watch Islamic extremism unravel countries in Africa and the Middle East, we are reminded that there is no easy formula for peace and progress in the world, but certainly if US money is being used a little more wisely toward that goal, it is partly the legacy of Henry Hyde.

I had once considered becoming a lawyer and thus had always found some joy in working alongside attorneys, even when it was costing me hundreds of dollars an hour. The House Judiciary Committee is the only committee we have for overseeing the proper administration of justice throughout the federal court system, and what it does can touch the life of every American. It is, quite plainly, "the Committee of the Constitution."

I came to the committee just as Henry was passing the gavel to Representative Jim Sensenbrenner (R-WI). Jim was like Henry in many ways: a staunch conservative, perhaps with a bit more of a libertarian streak. Jim's size, red cheeks, and good nature also make him an imposing figure. He's not particularly soft-spoken—and can be dictatorial when he needs to be—but is both warm and skilled at casting off attempts to demean him.

Under the umbrella of the Judiciary Committee, I would go on to serve on the Subcommittee on Commercial and Administrative Law and the Subcommittee on Regulatory Reform, Commercial and Antitrust Law. Fourteen years later, also under Judiciary, I would eventually chair the subcommittee that I had set my sights on back in 2001: the Subcommittee on Courts, Intellectual Property and the Internet, combining my love of technology and my love-hate fascination with law.

In between those times, though, I would serve as ranking member and later chair of the committee that would change my life, my public profile, and, for good or ill, my view of how government functions. The Committee on Oversight and Government Reform would prove to be the site of some of the most important political battles of recent years.

One unsettling fact made clear while I was still ranking member was that business and government certainly do mix in Washington, but not necessarily in beneficial ways.

In 2008, we learned of the ways Countrywide Financial Corporation had maintained a so-called VIP and "Friends of Angelo" program, by which certain favored government officials—who were in a position to assist Countrywide in regulatory matters— were given mortgage financing at unusually favorable rates. Countrywide CEO Angelo Mozilo was the "Angelo," and he was collecting friends in government and industry. It was all so brazen, seemingly ripped straight from a script for a show such as *House of Cards*. But it was happening for real—and no one seemed willing to try to stop it.

I wrote several letters urging greater disclosure of the potential scandal and pushed the Democrat majority of the committee to pursue it much more aggressively.

Our initial investigation uncovered troubling details and indications of even far worse things—from both Republicans and Democrats. We pressed ahead anyway. After much prodding by myself and others, the Oversight Committee chairman at the time, Representative Ed Towns (D-NY), issued the first subpoena in 2009.

What we ultimately discovered was breathtaking.

Between January 1996 and June 2008, Countrywide's VIP loan unit made a large number of loans to current and former members of Congress, congressional staff, high-ranking government officials, and executives and employees of the Federal National Mortgage Association (widely known as Fannie Mae), including Chairmen James Johnson, Franklin Raines, and Daniel Mudd. Other VIPs who worked at Fannie Mae enjoyed expedited loan processing and pricing discounts.

If that isn't wrong, I don't know that Washington can understand what is right.

Countrywide also waived company guidelines for Fannie Mae's senior executives to a greater extent than it did for "regular" VIPs. The unit also processed loans for key senators and Senate staff who could be helpful, giving VIP loans to Senator Chris Dodd, Senate Budget Committee Chairman Kent Conrad, and Mary Jane Collipriest, communications director for former Senator Robert Bennett, who served on the Committee on Banking, Housing, and Urban Affairs. In fact, Dodd referred Collipriest to the VIP unit.

As Senator Bennett had been instrumental in killing legislation suggested by the Bush administration to rein in Fannie Mae and restrict its reckless activities, it was, to me, a clear example of how corrupt lobbying sinks reform legislation.

The company also forged relationships with members and staff of the House of Representatives. The VIP unit processed loans for some of my colleagues, including Buck McKeon and Elton Gallegly.

Though it's hardly surprising that a program designed to curry favor with Washington insiders would include some members of Congress, Ed Towns's issuance of that first subpoena was notable because he himself had received a loan through the VIP program. I always found Ed to be a good and fair person, and he demonstrated it there.

Countrywide also did special favors for key decision makers in the executive branch. Two former secretaries of housing and urban development—Alphonso Jackson and Henry Cisneros—received VIP loans. The VIP unit processed Cisneros's loan after he joined the company's board of directors. Jim Johnson referred former secretary of health and human services Donna Shalala to the VIP unit as well.

Why did a vision of pigs at the trough keep coming to mind?

It should be mentioned that some serviced by the VIP unit, such as my friend Congressman Pete Sessions (R-TX) specifically sought and received no special treatment. That was documented in Countrywide's own files.

By contrast, McKeon, later chairman of the House Committee on Armed Services, not only denied he had received a VIP loan when he had, but internal Countrywide emails describe him as "a bit difficult to deal with. He seems on the edgy side."

The names listed above, "Friends of Angelo," VIPs, and others in government who sought and received preferential treatment, represent a specific, serious, and *bipartisan* problem in Washington. They were both Democrats and Republicans, representing diverse backgrounds, experiences, and stations of life. It is galling to think that when the nation entrusts a handful of legislators and regulators with so much power, there is sometimes little to ensure they will use that power wisely or that they will not be tempted to take advantage of the system and enrich themselves.

Another fundamental point: I believe the "Friends of Angelo" program also likely contributed in a very direct way to the 2008 financial crisis.

Countrywide was constantly persuading friendly politicians to avoid greater regulatory restrictions on Fannie Mae and Freddie Mac, which became federal mortgage-backing and mortgage-securitizing entities. The fact that both of them enlarged their role in the runaway housing market shielded them from exactly the kind of oversight that might have stopped it.

Instead, Fannie and Freddie were ultimately to be found at the heart of the financial meltdown. That is the intoxicating power and corrosive effect of big government and big business joining together and exchanging favors.

Rarely have insider dealing and institutional corruption had bigger consequences for public policy or done greater damage to individual Americans and the national economy.

CHAPTER SIX

The Recall Election and the Rise of the Terminator

Many regarded the 2003 recall of California governor Gray Davis as a political oddity. Others have concluded that the gubernatorial administration of Arnold Schwarzenegger was a failure, given his rocky term in office. But that is an incomplete assessment that fails to capture the enormity of the event, the scope of what it accomplished, and the exhilarating way that Californians truly held their leaders accountable and took back their government. It was a pure and powerful example of the type of accountability that voters consistently say they prefer and too few in government get to experience. The recall started as an idea, became a cause, and spawned a movement. And it didn't stop until it had overturned the entire political establishment of the largest state in America.

Under the governorship of Gray Davis, the lights were literally going off all over California—a man-made disaster played out on the public power grid. At first Davis had ignored the warning signs of the state's volatile electricity market. Then he began a series of frenzied moves, leading to energy supply failures, contributing to a staggering state budget crisis, and resulting in a drastic loss of public confidence.

Though it was not all the fault of any one person, it was a clear example of a harmful instinct of both the elected governor and the unelected permanent government bureaucracy: faced with a large problem, to design creative excuses, discover convenient scapegoats, and, at all costs, avoid responsibility. Though this kind of buck-passing occurs practically every day at every level of government, it can, on occasion, careen out of control. That is what happened in California.

In my view, following eight years of steady Pete Wilson as the state's chief executive, certain people in California, such as Gray Davis, concluded that governing must be easy: you just sit back, wait for the revenue to roll in, and figure out how to spend it. No tough decisions, no thorny problems, no need to stray from the status quo. That aloofness came back to bury Davis, who was totally unprepared for trouble both from a policy standpoint and from a personal perspective. He refused to level with the public about the unforeseen aspects of the electricity crisis and was too slow in acting to fix it. Californians paid dearly for Davis's missteps.

He managed to be reelected in 2002 but with only 47.4 percent of the vote in what was also one of the lowest turnout elections in history—a far cry from the popular landslide that had swept him into office four years earlier. Even so, he still could have eluded his ultimate political fate. But, perhaps flush from winning reelection, he betrayed the public that had given him a second chance by declaring no substantial change in course and undertaking several actions that infuriated the already skeptical voters.

Also, shortly after being sworn in for a second term, Davis revealed that the state's budget deficit could be as much as $35 billion—even though only weeks earlier he had said it would be far less. Ultimately, the state's books were deemed to be more than $38 billion in the red, more than all of the other forty-nine states combined.

The recall rumblings followed soon after.

A Sacramento-based antitax activist named Ted Costa was the first to be approved by state election officials to gather petitions for a recall of Davis. He was joined by some others—including talk radio hosts—but no real headway was made. The public sentiment against Davis was strong, but that would not be enough to remove him from office.

Most daunting to the scrappy bunch trying to achieve a recall was that they required nearly 900,000 petition signatures by early September. In political terms, it was an almost superhuman feat, and it was not going to happen without more resources than they could muster.

I convened a team of my closest advisers at the time and put them to work on the main questions of the matter: Could this be done? Should we try to lead it publicly? Who would run for governor in the election that would occur simultaneously with the vote to decide if Davis should be removed from office? Would this completely distract from (or perhaps even end) my career in Congress, which was just beginning?

I decided to help.

First, I was still closely following California state government and politics at the time and was truly alarmed at how much—and how quickly—the state had slipped in the Davis years. Far from the many natural disasters that can plague California, what ailed the state at the time was an outbreak of poor leadership and a refusal to deal honestly with a public whose suffering was increasing the longer the crisis went on.

California matters. It's a national bellwether, and it can influence the nation at large in both good ways and bad. This was bad. My adopted home state (the place where my family and I had been blessed to live and work for years) was truly reeling under governmental chaos: record budget deficits and now the lights literally flickering from San Diego to San Francisco—when they weren't going out altogether. Davis proved to be simply overwhelmed by the task. I believed very strongly that things in Sacramento weren't going to improve. California's condition would continue to decline, and the climate was right to make a change.

Before undertaking the recall, we didn't even take a poll. We didn't conduct a focus group. But we had a sense, different from that of many experts, that it was time to ditch not only Davis but the system he oversaw—perhaps opening up the process to someone outside of the traditional governing class.

After all, if the "most prepared governor in history" (as Davis called himself) had been proven not to be up to the job, the voters had every right to opt for another kind of leader and to demand a different way of leading the state.

For a while, I considered running myself, and for the several months in which we simultaneously championed the recall as well as the petition drive to make it a ballot reality, I was one of the only elected officials doing it publicly. As I came to find out, many in the Republican camp were not just undecided—but opposed to Davis's removal from office.

In retrospect, I believe that Republicans should have pulled together early in the process to try to determine who the GOP's most likely candidates would be in the event of a recall. But that did not come close to happening.

As summer approached, Davis was spending considerable time blaming the Bush administration for his troubles, saying that Dick Cheney himself was instrumental in supporting the recall and proclaiming that national Republicans were gunning for him.

If he only knew! Practically everyone in the Republican establishment wanted me to stop—and told me so many times.

While Davis was summoning the national Democrat machine to help him (and attack me), there were grumblings that the White House did not welcome the recall effort. I requested a meeting with top Bush political adviser Karl Rove to sort it out. Interestingly, it was Rove's deputy, Ken Mehlman, who took the meeting, and it did not appear to be a last-minute change of plans. Karl apparently concluded that the conversation didn't rise to his level.

Mehlman quickly got to the point: we should cease and desist with the recall, and if we didn't, there could be hell to pay.

Why? Ultimately, they did not believe that the recall would succeed. Even my California congressional colleague David Dreier, who would go on to head Schwarzenegger's transition team, wanted me to stop and warned me against proceeding.

The political calculations from Republicans trying to stop us went something like this: a wounded Gray Davis would provide a genuine opportunity to showcase failed Democrat policies and do it at a time that might provide a much more fertile political ground for President Bush's re-election in 2004.

That might be, but a "wounded" Davis had also severely harmed the economic and industrial structure of my state and was hurting it more all the time. Weren't there better ways to persuade the people of California to vote Republican than just waiting for things to get manifestly worse?

That is not to say that Rove or Mehlman or Dreier didn't know what they were talking about. They are all political experts. And they were right to emphasize the fact that only one other governor in the entire country had been recalled from office—in North Dakota in 1921. Many had been targeted over the following eighty-two years, and every one had withstood the challenge. What made us think this recall was even possible, let alone probable?

Disagreeing with friends is never easy, and this was no exception. But in this case, declining their advice (to say nothing of their threats) was not a tough call. Though I was respectful of the opinion of the Bush White House, its top political people, and my colleagues in Congress, they simply were not seeing from Washington, DC, what I was seeing in every corner of California. But they were right about one thing: they had warned me that I would be taken to task for the recall, and they were surely right, although perhaps not in the way they intended.

The full force of the governor of California, national Democratic political organizations, and practically every liberal special interest joined forces and started blasting away—not at our challenges to Davis's record of failure but at me and my family. It was brutal.

Practically every day—and often every hour—a new barrage would appear. Questions planted in the media about my high school years, my grades there and in college, my brothers, my wife, her family, our business, my work associates—it was all put in the worst way and under the brightest lights possible. I was called a criminal, corrupt, dangerous. The campaign to tear me down was not subtle.

Political ads targeting me by name started popping up all over the airwaves. Shadowy groups (including StopIssa.org) took to the Internet to spread false rumors and outright lies, even featuring an image of a faceless criminal pointing a gun straight at you, with the message "Don't let DARRELL ISSA hijack California's election process!"

One of the most prominent radio commercials of the group said, "A guy comes up to you on the street, sticks a petition in your face, and asks you to sign . . . so the next time you see Darrell Issa or one of his petitions in your neighborhood, lock your car [and] get your kids in the house."

The reality on the ground was far different. Everywhere we offered petitions, people signed them. I remember that one family brought their small children to one of our locations "to show our kids this is what democracy looks like." It doesn't get more meaningful than that. Many individuals even collected signatures from their friends and neighbors and sent them to us. It was inspiring. That sort of thing simply doesn't happen.

Far from hijacking anything, it was the people themselves who were taking control by exercising their constitutional rights in our democracy.

Though the attempt to destroy my reputation made things very hard on my staff and my friends and family—including my elderly mother and young son—if it was intended to intimidate me into backing down, it backfired spectacularly. I certainly didn't like the experience of being targeted by biased media reporters and the attack professionals working for Davis. Of course, I heard some of the attack ads. But I knew that by going after me, the other side was revealing the central weakness of the case against the recall. If they could have beaten us by defending the Davis record, they would have. They couldn't—so they didn't. They just threw the kitchen sink at me.

Still, the act that proved to be just about the most damaging to anyone's reputation during this time was something Davis did all on his own.

On June 20, 2003, Davis tripled the state's vehicle license fee, known to drivers everywhere as the "car tax." That infuriated drivers in car-friendly California, who didn't appreciate being sent the bill for Sacramento's mismanagement of state finances and had proof in their mailboxes that that was exactly what was happening.

Almost from the moment the car tax increase was announced and people started receiving higher bills than they were expecting (and knew why), we saw a sharp increase in support for the recall. By the time Davis himself advanced a plan to *reverse* the car tax increase, he pulled off the rare feat of looking both unwise and uncertain.

As unlikely as it must have seemed to the White House—and as historically unprecedented as it was—the fact is that the recall of Gray Davis was popular, pronounced, and gaining steam. People had joined up and were working hard, and we were seeing results. How could I abandon them?

We ended up getting almost a half-million more signatures than were required, and in about half the time allotted by the rules. It was a highly professional effort, to be sure, but it was also helped by a surge in citizen involvement not seen before (if ever) and unnoticed by many in politics and the media—though it surely hid in plain sight.

Ultimately, as it became clear that the recall was going to qualify for the ballot, Arnold Schwarzenegger entered the race, and it was immediately apparent to me that it was his time. The dynamic combination of his immigrant success story, good-natured celebrity image, well-known civic involvement, and many business accomplishments fused together perfectly with the moment—and the movement. In that political environment, he was an excellent fit.

Still, many encouraged me to run for governor, even though that was not my plan and it wasn't why we had done the recall. I had invested in it to make a decisive difference for California and transform (at least for a while) its political and governmental landscape.

As I made the public announcement in San Diego that the recall was indeed going to happen and that I would not be a candidate for governor, the enormity of what we had accomplished—and what it would mean for the future—instantly became apparent. I knew my life would never be the same, nor would my career in Congress. It was an emotional moment, with Kathy at my side and surrounded by so many loyal and devoted supporters. Some were in tears. I was deeply moved.

Immediately after that poignant press conference, as I sat in my car in the adjacent parking area with Kathy and two campaign staffers, everyone was still. I knew deep down that this was a cause for celebration, not sadness, but it had still been a long and draining day.

My communications director broke the tension in the silent and still unmoving car: "Does this mean we're not going to Sacramento?"

We all laughed, drove on, and began the final twists and turns of the recall experience.

I've joked since then that from that day on and for most of the next four months, I never took off my makeup from TV appearances, going on everything from local television affiliates to Fox News to ABC and seemingly everywhere in between. It was that way all the way through to the October election day—selling people on why the recall represented the legitimate will of the people and why Arnold was the best man for the job.

In the final days of the campaign, as Schwarzenegger barnstormed the state and invited me to join him and speak at every stop, we were witness to a massive and sweeping authentic public demand for accountability in government. Davis had stood in the way, so the people had removed him. Schwarzenegger embodied their hopes, so they elected him.

It's important to note that a higher percentage of Californians cast their votes in the 2003 recall than in the 2002 general election the year before. That simply demolishes the argument that the recall was illegitimate due to the fact that it took place in an election "off-year."

Also, despite an almost obscene amount of media attention to many of the colorful and bizarre candidates that appeared on the ballot that year to replace Davis, more than 94 percent of all ballots were cast for the top three candidates: Schwarzenegger received 49 percent of the vote, Democratic lieutenant governor Cruz Bustamante gained 32 percent and 13 percent voted for Republican Tom McClintock (now a fellow member of Congress).

The voters knew exactly what they were doing.

California has a great love affair with ballot initiatives and views them—correctly in my view—as quintessentially democratic and empowering of the people. I fear that those who hold power in politics will always seek ways to make it more difficult for citizen movements to access the ballot. If they'd been able to, they would have stopped the recall cold.

In the end, I'm enormously proud of what was accomplished. Despite all the attacks on me (some even by my supposed political allies) as well as all that my family had to endure, we would do it all over again. To this day, I'm still stopped in airports or restaurants and thanked for making the recall a reality. Words can't describe how rewarding that is.

The real credit belongs to the people—but I'm happy to have done my part and grateful for the support of those who believe it made California a better place and struck a blow for accountability everywhere.

CHAPTER SEVEN

Second Thoughts on Six Years with the Fourth Estate

M ore than a decade later, in 2015, I would watch many of my House Republican colleagues express their dissatisfaction with Speaker of the House John Boehner. It's probably safe to say that amid the harsh criticisms directed at him, few recalled that back in 2009, he had a unique instinct for and farsighted analysis of political press strategy and the media landscape. But he did.

In 2009, Republicans were still despondent due to the elections of 2006 and 2008—and with good reason.

In the 2006 elections, the GOP lost control of both the House and the Senate in a national landslide defeat. Two years later, not only was Barack Obama elected in a decisive victory that put the White House into the Democrats' control, but Republicans, already in the minority, lost even more seats in the House and Senate. We put a brave face on things, but privately, many were discouraged, even distraught. Who could blame them?

Then the House minority leader, Boehner surveyed the political environment (and our much smaller ranks) and offered an assessment that was crucial for us going forward: "From this point, we transitioned from legislating to *communicating*."

That is not to say we were told to shirk our responsibilities as lawmakers. Nor did it mean that we could not affect and improve any aspect of the legislative process, even though we were essentially powerless (and made even more so by Nancy Pelosi's exclusionary rules when she was Speaker of the House, which completely stifled fair discussion).

I took what Boehner was saying to mean that the Republicans had been put into the position of the loyal opposition. We had to do something about it, and the best and fastest way to succeed was to reach the public by telling our story, explaining our objections, pointing out better ideas—and doing it all through media that were, at that point, providing Barack Obama the kind of honeymoon some married couples only dream about.

Sounded easy enough.

At that point, we weren't thirsting to be back in power; we were just hungry for relevance. And public awareness was our guiding goal. For the Oversight Committee, it made perfect sense. We were not the Republican National Committee.

I decided that Boehner was correct, and although not every one of my House colleagues seemed to buy into it, on the Oversight Committee we set about emphasizing communications in our work. Still, there was no template to follow, no precedent for the kind of committee we wanted to structure and the kind of oversight we needed to perform.

Primarily, we would devote unprecedented resources to media relations and redirect the focus of both our press representatives *and* staffers who did not normally deal directly with the media. They would now be part of "communications" as well.

For example, not only were writers and press staff tasked with preparing the maximum number possible of editorials, op-eds, and other related communications content, every staff member of the committee (including investigators) was expected to contribute to the drafting and preparation of those materials.

We got early wins, and they brought the team together. The top communicator on my staff, Frederick Hill, says, "By being aggressive and challenging things, we proved that even the minority could break through. It was a meaningful accomplishment—and to the media, a validation of our work, too."

That was at a time of considerable media consolidation and a historic diminishment of the print world. Newspapers and newsmagazines were shrinking, first in size, then, inevitably, in influence.

A simultaneous transition took place to the virtual world of the online stage. Gone in an instant was the era of column inches, early-afternoon deadlines, and "putting the paper to bed." Now we were in an era of unlimited available space, anytime access to reporters, and a culture of the infinite deadline. This content-driven, ever-changing, cable/online media environment spawned more journalists and journalism than ever. It also provided an open forum for eager, energetic reporters with new voices to be heard, no longer shut out by the gatekeepers of the nation's prestigious journalism schools.

As for the professional journalists who survived the tumult, their jobs changed, too. Now many of them were asked to report on and complete one story every day and sometimes more—making an aspect of their craft less a methodical search for a story and more often an exercise in journalism by the pound.

That meant information was still a currency, but with a much different value. There might have been more information than ever and fewer traditional places to deliver it—but new portals had also popped up. And they were endlessly voracious. Realizing we were in a twenty-four-hour news cycle, we started feeding as many of those twenty-four hours as we could. And sometimes we fed them all.

Some will view this as a commitment to "spin"—the exercise of media manipulation, robotic message discipline, and twisting of the truth—but that's not what we were up to. We reached the obvious conclusion that if we didn't present and fight with facts, truth, and information unearthed by our oversight work, we would be quickly disarmed and ultimately unsuccessful.

Though I recognize that the House of Representatives is a political environment, the truth is that, much like the rest of the federal government, it contains very antiquated and even duplicative systems. That was not at all conducive to the new information age, and it showed.

Six years ago, not only were iPhones not approved House devices (we were issued only BlackBerry devices), but many of my House colleagues did not utilize fast-moving and far-reaching social media. They were of course happy to put out a supportive press release, as long as you gave them an entire day to get it done. I appreciated the care and diligence with which they were doing their work, but the newly impatient media were positioned for and available to someone to approach them and try to persuade them. If we weren't first in line, we believed that not only might we not just be last, but we might not get an audience at all.

So we resolved first for the committee to transition from an information-based entity to a communications-based organization. That was a change from the everyday because some congressional committees traditionally build huge bureaucracies that require multiple sign-offs even on some of the most mundane matters. Though this has traditionally contributed to a sort of institutional power, it is based on anything but the need for speed.

By contrast, we were racing sixty-five miles per hour where the speed limit had been twenty-five as long as anyone could remember. Some thought we should slow down, but we just kept flooring it.

What we employed was the hustle and efficiency of the campaign environment, which can be frantic even on the most under-control days. Because campaigns are terminal events that end on election day and are decided by a vast audience of which you can reach only a tiny portion, they are compelled to move fast, be concise, and do it every day.

Therefore, the inherent nature of our work didn't change; it instead became infused with a commitment to produce material that was meaningful—but also understandable. We knew we had to be not just right or correct but also fast and first. Being first was unusual in the congressional atmosphere. Congress was not traditionally set up as a place conducive to rapid response (or even a same-day callback), and not only in the press shop. But if our committee's investigations required a subpoena, our staff and attorneys could now have it ready in less than a day. That was unheard of.

When political professionals say "Speed kills," they mean it in a much different way than the highway patrol does. For a while, it became our guiding principle. For us, speed "killed" when it determined the course the media followed in reporting our investigations. It set the tone and tenor of the conversation and, as much as anything else, allowed us to have our voice heard at a time when Republicans throughout Washington were practically muted.

Soon, however, we noticed that the media were increasingly interested in what those of us on "the other side" were saying. If we made an accusation about ACORN or Countywide or another scandal and the accusations were founded and justified, reporters started to ask: Why aren't the majority Democrats and the Obama administration asking basic questions and trying to find out the truth?

In those early skirmishes, if we got there first, it was our accusation, then their rebuttal. We liked those terms because, as the adage goes, in politics if you're explaining, you're losing. At the time, we were doing a lot of accusing, and the Obama administration was doing most of the explaining.

We were under no misconceptions that the media were friendly to us or on our side. We knew that many of the Beltway journalists had been outright cheerleaders for the White House and that most were at least reflexively supportive of Obama and his programs. As a matter of routine, they would and did take everything we provided and ran straight to the White House, or one of the departments or agencies we were investigating, and ask for comment to generate headline-grabbing content.

Fair enough. We understood they had a job to do (a very new job for some of them), and as they were figuring out their way, we were happy to oblige. We also kept it simple; we didn't have the resources of the executive branch of the White House helping us, so we were compelled to be as interesting and as easily understood as possible—and win the "volume" game.

To be sure, we have had plenty of disagreements with the media. But that was an important lesson in how to understand and anticipate sound ways to unveil real news and inform a national audience hungry for information. It required an approach that was comprehensive, detailed, and get-it-done-right; others were condensed, cursory, and get-it-done-yesterday. It worked very well. At one point, committee staff drove three major investigations simultaneously and distinctively with three to four days of media narrative and comprehensive conversation planned out in advance.

It wasn't substantially different from being back running my business: as long as there were customers in line, I had to make sure they all got served.

This combined approach produced nontraditional press releases without the usual clever headlines and quick-hitting sound bites. They contained entire paragraphs (or even pages) of information and were backed up by much more than that: committee reports that were many pages long, meticulously detailed, and containing hard facts.

Our media delivery was no data dump, though; it was a finely honed process. It wouldn't have worked any other way. We gained press access, solid placement, and consistent credibility because our material wasn't just interesting, it was accurate. What it lacked in conciseness, we made up for in comprehensiveness.

That is why the Obama administration initially did not know how to react to what we were doing. We couldn't be dismissed as lacking substance. And we couldn't be countered with empty "spin."

Our lead committee investigator, Steve Castor, says, "We had to be meticulous about attaching evidence to every fact and adding foot-notes to every meaningful sentence of our reports because of media skepticism. But it was good thing. It earned us legitimacy, as well."

A couple of years earlier, the strategy would not have worked; there was too much information chasing too few outlets. But at this time, the media were ready for as much as we could give them, and we saw it happen in the first weeks of the Obama administration.

After the White House's first choice as secretary of commerce stepped aside, an intriguing selection emerged: Republican US

Senator Judd Gregg of New Hampshire, a fiscal conservative and independent-minded DC veteran. But almost immediately, our attention turned to a serious concern about the political motives of the White House. In retrospect, it was a revealing example of the aggressive partisan politics that would animate the entire Obama administration.

At the time, plans were being put in place for the director of the next year's census to report not to the secretary of commerce, as was the usual practice, but directly to the White House. "There's only one reason to have that high level of White House involvement," a career professional at the Census Bureau told the *Wall Street Journal* at the time. "And it's called politics, not science."

A politicized census count would have dramatic implications for our entire national elections system, and, if manipulated, could have helped Democrats gain an undue upper hand in the reapportionment system that redraws every congressional district in the country once every decade, according to census results.

It was the kind of "Chicago-style" politics we'd hoped we wouldn't see from this White House—but feared we would.

President Obama's calls for bipartisanship at that time were severely damaged by requiring the census director to report directly to White House Chief of Staff Rahm Emanuel. It was a shamefully transparent attempt to politicize the Census Bureau and manipulate the 2010 census, especially given that Emanuel was a former Democratic member of Congress and former head of the Democratic Congressional Campaign Committee. (He is now, not surprisingly, the mayor of Chicago.)

The Oversight Committee has jurisdiction over the census, and we went after the administration's plainly political power grab— particularly in the media, which pursued the story and amplified our concerns. As a result, only nine days after he was nominated, Senator Gregg withdrew as Obama's commerce secretary nominee. The census also remained out of the direct control of the White House.

Stepping back and surveying the aftermath, we realized we had been able to affect the outcome, not just by getting under people's skin but by affecting—and reversing—an official action.

Also in 2009, several members from various chapters of the social service group ACORN (Association of Community Organizations for Reform Now) were caught on video not only advising undercover videographers James O'Keefe and Hannah Giles in a way that seemed to condone illicit behavior, but advising them how to break the law as well.

ACORN was already known to many of us in Congress, and in February 2009, the Obama administration named ACORN a national partner with the Census Bureau to help recruit some of the one million temporary workers needed to go door to door to conduct the surveys.

Fox News disclosed that:

ACORN, which claims to be a non-partisan grassroots community organization of low- and moderate-income people, came under fire in 2007 when Washington State filed felony charges against several paid ACORN employees and supervisors for more than 1,700 fraudulent voter registrations. In March 2008, an ACORN worker in Pennsylvania was sentenced for making 29 phony voter registration forms. The group's activities were frequently questioned in the 2008 presidential election.[1]

Though I am sure the group's long and close ties to Barack Obama prior to his presidency were a factor in this story's gaining attention, the details about ACORN's misdeeds were just too damming.

As CNN reported at the time:

> The video shows the pair approaching two women working at the ACORN Baltimore office and asking them for advice on how to set up a prostitution ring involving more than a dozen underage girls from El Salvador.
>
> One of the ACORN workers suggests that Giles refer to herself as a "performing artist" on tax forms and declare some of the girls as dependents to receive child tax credits.
>
> "Stop saying prostitution," the woman, identified by the filmmaker as an ACORN tax expert, tells Giles. The other woman tells them, "You want to keep them clean . . . make sure they go to school."[2]

The story was made even bigger and lasted longer because our staff had already issued a report about ACORN's additional controversial activities, and the truth is that the organization had been on the wrong track for some time.

Ultimately, the House voted 345–75 and the Senate 85–11 to strip ACORN of federal funding—a rare bipartisan effort in both houses of Congress and a solid win for the taxpayers.

If the video was the spark to the wider public audience, our documents and report were the kindling. They were decisive on every front, including our media relations, because they proved we had the goods and had found the information through hard work and diligent investigation—and had done so outside of the bright lights. We were rewarded with considerable coverage, but the fact is, our team had earned it.

Soon after the story broke, ACORN staffers were fired, several of its state chapters shut their doors, and the next year, the organization filed for Chapter 7 bankruptcy and disbanded.

In very early 2010, we saw another payoff on another big stage with an even more prominent player.

We had obtained email messages that suggested the Federal Reserve Bank of New York had discouraged the financial giant AIG from revealing certain facts in its filings with the Securities and Exchange Commission about the government bailout it had received.

That reeked of a cover-up, and it pointed directly to Timothy Geithner, the former head of the New York Reserve Bank and the Obama administration's first secretary of the Treasury. Even many Democrats were concerned about what was so obviously an attempt to frustrate public accountability, and Geithner's contentious and evasive testimony raised a lot more questions than it answered.

In reporting this story, *Bloomberg Businessweek* titled it "Tim Geithner's Tormentor"—meaning me. A clever headline, to be sure, but the credit isn't mine. Any torment Geithner might have felt resulted only from his disingenuous answers to legitimate questions and the fact that the New York Fed that he had once headed had been caught red-handed attempting to keep from the public embarrassing things it didn't want anyone to know.

Still, what we were able to discover and disseminate to a larger audience was a sizable accomplishment and left its mark. Geithner's reputation was damaged by the facts that were uncovered. He limped through most of the rest of his term at Treasury and resigned before Obama's second term. I didn't notice that many of my colleagues—including Democrats—seemed sorry to see him go.

Looking back on the census controversy, the ACORN scandal, and the Geithner revelations, it proved that what our committee did in private work and public communications could combine to have a great and lasting impact.

Like many fast starts out of the blocks, though, we found it difficult to maintain the pace.

That was sometimes our own doing, but it happened just as often because of roadblocks and speed traps put into our path, some of them set up by our own side. Though it is true we were far from perfect, we were also routinely delayed by turf battles and jurisdictional quarrels—more often among Republicans than among Democrats. The resulting sit-down meetings droned on not just for hours but for days and even weeks.

Of course some people, including in my own party, criticized me for being too aggressive, called us reckless for conducting investigations that met dead ends or the occasional pothole, or thought we were prioritizing the wrong problems. But the extraordinary success we had in our investigations, the glimpse we gave the American people of the failings of their own government, would not have been possible without the tenacity we brought to the task and the media attention we were able to generate. Of that I am certain.

Through years of direct media relations, completing thousands of press interviews and meeting hundreds of journalists, my views of the media haven't really changed—about their power, their influence, their bias, or their necessity. The fourth estate is as necessary as the three branches of government, legislative, judicial, and executive. In their wisdom, the Founders provided the media both sweeping powers and special protections and made clear what they considered the most likely threat to a free press. That is why the words of the First Amendment are so unmistakable: "Congress shall make no law . . . abridging the freedom of speech, or of the press."

But with great protections and great power come perhaps even greater responsibility. The press is the direct and proper conduit between the powerful and the people. It's a most precious gift. At its best, it provides truths the people want to know and deserve to have. But it can also be severely compromised by the practice of producing nonstop news, in which a story starts out with the presenting of material facts but by the end of the day has devolved into hours of speculation and opinion.

For that reason, I welcome the emerging democratization of journalism in which genuine and great work is being done in so many different places—including expert analysis that was formerly limited to a few traditional media outlets. But that can get drowned out by the partisan noise and by *situational* analysis: Who's up? Who's down? And how did it play?

The habit of much of the media to act as a sort of enthusiastic boxing referee encouraging both sides to mix it up is a masquerade of impartiality and has definitely outlived its usefulness.

I thought longtime CBS newsman Bob Schieffer was a very good example of the best way to practice aggressive, inquisitive journalism without the rough edges and sharp elbows some believe are requisite to getting ahead. As someone who's been accused of being aggressive and impatient myself, I well understand the impulse of many television talking heads to think they can bombast their way to prominence.

They should watch a few Bob Schieffer clips. Clear and courtly in a Texas way, he never did an interview that I recall in which he interrupted in a rude way or interjected his own view where it clearly didn't belong. Though his questions of me were tough and challenging, I found him quite fair and actually interested in the answers, not just his own point of view. There doesn't have to be crude confrontation for the audience to gain information.

Contrast this with a broadcaster such as Candy Crowley. To most people, she will always be remembered for her shocking interruption during the second Obama/Romney debate, siding with the president and trading her position as moderator for that of Chief Protector of the Chief Executive.

Romney very accurately stated that weeks had passed before Obama called the deadly attacks in Benghazi, Libya, a terrorist attack.

Instead of letting the president answer for himself, she leaped to Obama's defense and said to the world, "He did call it an act of terror."

Is it any wonder that Obama then asked, "Can you say that a little louder, Candy?"

The fact is that it took more than two weeks of administration contortions before Obama admitted that Benghazi was a pre-planned terror assault—just as Romney claimed.

It was, perhaps, the most profound moment of media bias in US political history.

I had my own negative experience with Crowley.

At a time when we were investigating and disclosing widespread IRS wrongdoing that revealed disturbing truths about how the agency targeted innocent Americans, Crowley used our live CNN interview to confront me with little more than Democrat talking points. Worse, she would accuse *our committee*—not the IRS or the

White House—of withholding documents and not providing the whole story. I thought she misled every member of her limited television audience.

In our free society, Congress has no business trying to remake the media. Instead, the media are in the process of remaking government. Technology will see to that. A future of direct access to the public is coming in which both information and news will be available on demand and in real time to a wired world. If you can ask Siri for help or ask Uber for a ride, why can't you ask government for all the information you have a right to know? The traditional game of governmental hide-and-seek will eventually become impossible in the age of Google's search-and-find capability.

This may complicate the work of the media, but it is an opportunity to be seized, not a future to dread. Perhaps the press will have to compete with this enhanced public interest and public access—but it can also motivate and inspire the public who, as customers, will come out the big winners.

The media will have to be more thought-provoking as information becomes ubiquitous, and the ones that do it well stand to be rewarded handsomely in this new market. If you can imagine it today, it can likely be done today. If all things are possible, then most things are inevitable. But not everything is desirable. I believe the mainstream media will always be with us; it's the dominant, filtering function of the mainstream media that will go away.

Some of my fellow conservatives look at the dwindling readership of reliably liberal newspapers such as the *New York Times*, the *Washington Post*, and the *Los Angeles Times* and feel a sense of satisfaction. Others go even further, eagerly waiting the day when even the Gray Lady will shut her doors for good.

I understand the sentiment, but I cannot agree with it. The fact that the great majority of journalists and media professionals are liberal is a fact to be dealt with and called to account. We may not *like* the media, especially its institutional liberal bias. But we *need* the media—the best we can get.

CHAPTER EIGHT

Fast and Furious

The consequences of government making mistakes and not being held accountable are not just happy bureaucrats who get away scot free from their wrongdoing. Sometimes people die.

In our investigation of "Operation Fast and Furious," the "gun-walking" program in which the government allowed "straw purchasers" for Mexican gangs to buy guns that ended up being used in many crimes, my staff and I literally came face to face with the kind of unchecked arrogance that should trouble every American.

On June 19, 2012, my staff and I met privately with Attorney General Eric Holder. That was the night before the committee was scheduled to vote whether to recommend contempt of Congress charges against him for failure to turn over documents detailing the decision by senior Justice Department officials to lie to Congress about the Fast and Furious operation.

We had only two questions—and they were pretty simple:

- What had they known?
- And why had they lied?

Holder refused to provide the necessary documents that would answer the first question, and he flat out refused to tell anything like the full truth about the second.

We could have backed down and just groused about his lack of cooperation. But what we already knew about the scandal, and what we suspected we might still find out, made that option a nonstarter.

The meeting lasted less than half an hour, but we still made one last push to get him to turn over all relevant documents. My real dread was that he would feign cooperation and drag out the process through some phony semblance of compliance, all the while admitting to wearing "two hats," as he once put it: attorney general but also defender of the Obama administration. With this lofty if ambiguous role, he surely felt it an indignity to be pursued by cameras as he arrived for the meeting in the Capitol, appearing almost as if he were under indictment instead of the nation's chief law enforcement officer.

The Oversight staff and I had already resolved that we would not accept a bad deal just to help the administration make the Fast and Furious issue go away or even ease the concerns of some of our colleagues who were squeamish about holding the attorney general in contempt.

However, there were various possible reasonable deals that Holder might have offered that could have made the whole controversy go away. From the beginning of the investigation, when the Department of Justice had confirmed our sketchy "vignettes" describing the evolution of Fast and Furious, we had said, fine, give us all the emails related to these "vignettes" and they might suffice to answer our questions. The threat of a contempt vote against Holder would then vanish. The department had responded only with the vague offer of a few hundred self-selected emails it deemed a "fair compilation" of the Fast and Furious strategizing. Not even close to enough.

Tellingly, the DOJ had earlier intimated that the emails in question would not put the DOJ into a positive light. All we asked for was the chain of events and scope of conversations detailing events we knew had occurred and wanted to know the truth about.

We were also prepared to accept a deal whereby DOJ could promise to reform its procedures, which had led to the dangerous gun-walking being approved at the highest levels of the Justice Department, and we'd call off the contempt vote. Officials there said no.

Holder would not budge. The tension in the room was plain. A vein bulged in his neck, and it was clear that he was in no mood for further give and take. To my surprise, Deputy Attorney General James Cole presented the DOJ offer while Holder fumed. It was simply a repetition of the earlier offer: a sampling of emails in exchange for an end to the investigation. We were being asked to take his deal first and review some of the documents second.

Holder finally spoke up and told me it was a good deal and I should take it. I told him it was a deal he would never take—no competent prosecutor in the United States would accept a condition that allowed the subject of an investigation to withhold evidence.

To Holder, the meeting was just to check off a box on the list of perfunctory steps he'd have to pass through to put the affair behind him. He wanted it to be a certification that the investigation was over, an annoyance eliminated. He didn't seem to believe we'd press ahead with the contempt vote. The truth is, we were not certain that the Republican House leadership would actually back us up.

As committee chief counsel Steve Castor noted, Speaker Boehner would sign off on bringing a contempt vote only if Holder made
no serious attempt to resolve the impasse—and this meeting clearly
contained no attempt at resolution on Holder's part. "If they had
dumped another three hundred documents on us, it would have
delayed us," Castor said. "They could have buried us in 67,000 pages
if they wanted to."

But the DOJ didn't even pretend to cooperate. Holder simply
dared us to take action.

I actually found myself relaxing. Clearly, the Obama administration had badly miscalculated our willingness to go through with
a contempt vote. I already knew we had nearly all the Republican
members on the Oversight Committee willing to vote in favor.

This is an example of why government's mistakes must be
frankly addressed, investigated, and corrected. As in business, we
learn more from failures than from successes—if we are willing to
learn. Fast and Furious, it turned out, was a massive failure that had
involved *multiple* agencies, which can contribute to confusion. As
Steve learned in his trips into the field to talk to the agents involved,
when DEA agents arrived to observe some of the gun smug-
glers involved in Fast and Furious, they found Bureau of Alcohol,
Tobacco, Firearms and Explosives (ATF) agents already engaged in
long-term observation of the criminals—and wondered why they
hadn't yet made any arrests.

I have been fortunate during my time in Congress to be able to
observe political figures rising to power and falling from grace. The
recall election and the rise of Arnold Schwarzenegger, though serious business with big consequences for the state of California, was
an energizing, exhilarating experience that proved all is possible in
the cause of political reform and public accountability.

There was no great joy, though, in the high-profile conflict the Oversight Committee had with Holder, the roots of which grew out of events that transpired very early in Obama's presidency but culminated near the end of his first term with a historic rebuke of the nation's chief law enforcement officer and one of his most important appointees.

On June 28, 2012, a week after the committee vote, Holder became the first head of the Justice Department in history to be held in contempt by a congressional vote—one that most Democrats left the House floor to avoid, ostensibly walking off in protest, though they could easily have stayed and voted no. They should have voted yes.

Just as we all have a stake in being able to allow the public to recall an inept governor, surely we have a stake in ensuring that the highest-ranking appointee tasked with protecting our laws will himself obey them. If not, both the principle of governmental oversight and the rule of law become meaningless.

It may have been inevitable that the contempt vote on Holder would split mostly along party lines—another in the long line of strictly partisan actions driven by a White House that demanded Democrats stay in line, since Holder was too close to President Obama to risk offending the chief executive by condemning his closest ally. Even that power play was somewhat unsuccessful, as seventeen Democrats broke away and voted with us. They knew wrongdoing when they saw it.

But Holder's intentional withholding of documents from the Oversight Committee—to cover up earlier false statements Justice officials had provided to Congress about the Fast and Furious operation—was never just a partisan matter. It was a cover-up by the executive branch, treating the legislative branch as if the latter can be ignored. That my Democratic colleagues did not see this as a bipartisan concern could well have catastrophic long-term constitutional implications.

Holder is said by aides to have compared his testimony before the Oversight Committee to an appearance before a "wall of southern men." This patently false and racially loaded description may have (in his own mind) helped him dismiss the fact that he was criminally violating the laws he was charged to enforce, while protecting his own deputies, who had knowingly and willfully lied to Congress. Perhaps hurling undeserved racial invective our way salved his conscience or even the sting of contempt, but it is a coward's dodge at best.

My team and I did not set out to be divisive during my time as Oversight chairman. We sought only to pursue the truth—wherever it might have steered us. Sometimes the facts ensnared Republicans or put industries we supported into a bad light. That was as it should have been. To do our work, I recruited many talented fellow colleagues from the House. Representatives James Lankford (R-OK, now a senator), Mike Kelly (R-PA), Jim Jordan (R-OH), Trey Gowdy (R-SC), Dennis Ross (R-FL), and Pat Meehan (R-PA) were frequent allies.

Gowdy, a former prosecutor representing a conservative district, and Meehan, a former US attorney from a more moderate one, gave our committee a breadth of legal perspective not possible without both of them.

But often the Democrats, in a break with prior Oversight Committee tradition, stood in the way of even the most pressing investigations and the most obvious responsibilities of our job.

Even now, the sheer senselessness of Fast and Furious is difficult to comprehend. What's now very clear (and what we proved) is that Fast and Furious was at best criminally stupid, at worse fostered criminal acts in two countries, and worst of all metastasized into a near-top-to-bottom cover-up that obscured the truth about how an American law enforcement professional was killed.

What came to be known as Operation Fast and Furious grew out of a plan in which "straw purchasers" (essentially intermediary gun buyers functioning like mobile retailers utilizing wholesale operations) were permitted to buy large amounts of guns on the theory that the ATF would then be able to trace them to major drug cartels with the help of Mexican authorities. Some plan.

Within months of taking office, the Obama administration appears to have set to work on Fast and Furious. Instead of attempting to interdict illegally and suspiciously purchased weapons, DOJ and ATF would simply let the arms flow, even allowing them to be used in crimes and ostensibly planning to crack down on the criminals later. Law enforcement appeared to focus more attention on the US gun sellers, many of them actively encouraged by the government to make these bulk sales, than on monitoring the Mexican criminal cartels originally targeted.

Part of the plan was also to let a ring of straw purchasers, mostly in Arizona, buy guns and operate with minimal surveillance, then check to see if the guns reemerged at crime scenes. They did.

For a year, despite the objections of many ATF agents, weapons flowed into the hands of Mexican drug gangs. And because some of the straw purchasers in question were in a car club, the ATF program came to be called Operation Fast and Furious, after the successful movie and sequel franchise of the same name. All the while, ATF-facilitated gun sales were contributing to deaths along the crime-ravaged US-Mexico border and, according to Mexican authorities, were involved in numerous cases of Mexican civilians being injured or killed. Through it all, the Justice Department in Washington was hanging back and watching it all unfold.

Fast and Furious never came close to dismantling a drug cartel, but it did result in the indictments of approximately twenty straw purchasers. For their part, gun sellers who were cooperating with ATF actually expressed their reluctance to keep selling weapons to suspicious straw purchasers. Contrary to the image gun sellers have in the minds of some regulators and liberals, they usually have a feel for their customers and aggressively enforce existing gun laws (even if they are skeptical of new antigun regulations).

Yet ATF continued to assure the licensed gun sellers that all was well, that they should not worry about the absence of trackers that could be used to find the guns after they were sold to criminals, and that they should continue selling to what were obvious proxies for dangerous Mexican drug gangs.

Tragically, on December 14, 2010, a little more than a year into DOJ's gun-walking program, guns bought by straw purchaser Jaime Avila, Jr., were used to shoot and kill a Border Patrol agent named Brian Terry during a gun battle eighteen miles north of the Arizona/ Mexico border. Now that the program had gone terribly wrong— and had accomplished so little—one might expect that both ATF and DOJ would come clean about it and shut it down as a terribly flawed idea with deadly consequences. I certainly would have welcomed that explanation and apology.

But that's not what happened.

Instead, an administration-wide cover-up ensued as DOJ attempted to wash its hands of the whole program and make sure no one in Congress ever found out. First, despite many ATF agents voicing concerns about the guns vanishing untraced into the border gangland, DOJ higher-ups maintained that they were unaware of the problem. Attorney General Eric Holder would go a step farther and swear that he had not been aware of the Fast and Furious Operation at all. It was reasonable for the Oversight Committee to request related emails to see how far up the chain of command awareness of the program went.

We eventually found out the answer: all the way to the top.

By late January 2010, just three months after Fast and Furious had been conceived (and one year into the Obama presidency), the ATF Phoenix Field Division applied for Fast and Furious to become an Organized Crime Drug Enforcement Task Forces case, allowing for interagency coordination and a large increase in funding. It was to be a major group effort.

The US Attorney's Office in Arizona would run Fast and Furious and would oversee the combined efforts of ATF, the FBI, the Drug Enforcement Administration, the IRS, and Immigration and Customs Enforcement—all while reporting directly to the Department of Justice. Every step of the way, congressional oversight and understanding of this reality was thwarted and obscured.

What we eventually came to know was this: Only after two Fast and Furious guns were found at the site of Border Patrol agent Terry's death in December did the US attorney indict the straw purchasers. Yet more than a year earlier, in September 2009—according to emails from that time that would later be sought out by the Oversight Committee—the Department of Justice showed great interest in a prior gun-walking project and appeared to understand its dangers. DOJ prosecutor Laura Gwinn, of the Criminal Division's Organized Crime and Gang Section, emailed James Trusty, a senior official in the same section, to tell him, "Case involves 300 to 500 guns . . . It is my understanding that a lot of these guns 'walked.' Whether some or all of that was intentional is not known." An email from Trusty around that time also suggested that Assistant Attorney General Lanny Breuer was "VERY interested" in such a gun-walking program.

In December 2009, Acting ATF Director Kenneth Melson emailed DOJ's Breuer to say, "We have decided to take a little different approach with regard to seizures of multiple weapons in Mexico. Assuming the guns are traced, instead of working each trace almost independently of the other traces from the seizure, I want to coordinate and monitor the work on all of them collectively as if the seizure was one case."

Breuer responded, "We think this is a terrific idea and a great way to approach investigations of these seizures. Our Gang Unit will be assigning an attorney to help you coordinate this effort." Kevin Carwile, Chief of the DOJ Gang Unit, assigned attorney Joe Cooley to help with Fast and Furious for the next three months. Cooley received regular briefings and advised lead federal prosecutor Emory Hurley. Breuer himself met about the case with ATF officials, including William Hoover and Assistant Director for Field Operations Mark Chait.

Eric Holder's DOJ knew that Fast and Furious was going on, knew about prior problems with programs of this kind, and knew that the same ATF field division leaders were involved, now in an even looser and wider-open operation—and several officials had been briefed in March 2010 about the flow of Fast and Furious guns to Mexican cartels.

Memos from Breuer were included with each application (to his DOJ colleagues at the Office of Enforcement Operations) for the use of a wiretap in Fast and Furious. Three deputy assistant attorneys general at DOJ's Criminal Division signed off on the wiretap applications for Breuer. The reports of investigation used to construct those applications were among the thousands of documents withheld by DOJ when the Oversight Committee began inquiring about how and when DOJ had become aware of Fast and Furious.

Those documents would have revealed the detailed coordination between DOJ and the ATF operation in Arizona.

In fact, on March 12, 2010, Associate Deputy Attorney General Edward Siskel and then-acting Deputy Attorney General Gary Grindler received a thorough briefing on Fast and Furious that included a chart naming thirty-one straw purchasers and the weapons they had purchased to date (1,026, always using cash). Three purchasers had already bought more than a hundred each, one of them more than three hundred. A map of Mexico at that meeting showed the locations of crime scenes and stash houses stretching well south of the border.

By year's end, the operation would lead to Brian Terry's death—and he would not be the last. Fast and Furious–facilitated carnage continues on both sides of the border.

If the ATF, the US Attorney's Office, and midlevel DOJ officials were not taking responsibility for the Fast and Furious mess, the Oversight Committee could at least subpoena the numerous interagency and internal DOJ emails about how the mess had unfolded. At first, Senate Judiciary Committee ranking member Chuck Grassley (R-IA) and I, on behalf of the House Oversight Committee, requested documents about Fast and Furious from the ATF on March 16, 2011. It did not comply.

The press got slightly better results—the Mexican press, that is—eleven days later, when President Obama was asked on Mexican television whether he or US Attorney General Eric Holder were aware of Operation Fast and Furious. Obama said no, and at this point, Holder might have become committed to the lie that he was unaware of the whole thing. He was foolish to go down that path.

The US press, meanwhile, was inclined to let the whole matter slide and not pester the Obama administration with too many questions—with a few notable exceptions, including then–CBS reporter Sharyl Attkisson, who, like us, relied in large part on the goodwill of ATF insiders sickened by the behavior of some of their colleagues. In her book *Stonewalled: My Fight for Truth Against the Forces of Obstruction, Intimidation, and Harassment in Obama's Washington*, about pursuing highly sensitive stories against administration resistance, she recounts using sources "including six veteran ATF agents and executives who don't want to be quoted by name for fear of retaliation." She recounted having to coax info about the case out of a woman dating an ATF agent who called Attkisson out of the blue to report meekly, "My boyfriend wants to talk to you. . . . He has information about the story you've been working on." The committee knew very well what it was like to rely on frightened people to expose government's misdeeds.

We continued to be denied access to thousands of relevant documents, but Holder had appeared before the House Judiciary Committee on May 3 and claimed that only within the past few weeks had he heard about Fast and Furious. However, even with thousands of relevant emails still being withheld from Oversight investigators, a memo to Holder about Fast and Furious from a year earlier was discovered. Yet only in November 2011 would he even admit to the Senate Judiciary Committee, that any gun walking had occurred as part of Fast and Furious. (Strangely, he did appear to leak to the press an apologetic email to the Terry family—*before* sending it to them. Politico reported the contents of the email, after which the

Daily Caller reported that friends of the Terry family said the family themselves hadn't yet seen the message.)

By early 2012, Holder insisted before the House Judiciary Committee that DOJ was not engaging in a cover-up about Fast and Furious. Yet thousands of emails were still being kept from the Oversight Committee—which was how it was covering it up. On June 20, 2012, the Oversight Committee voted 23–17 to hold the attorney general of the United States, who was withholding documents, in contempt. A week later, on June 28, the House of Representatives affirmed our vote, even as a large portion of the Democratic representatives walked off the floor and exited the building, putting on a show of refusing to dignify the vote—while in fact evading the responsibility of going on record and casting a no vote if they really disagreed with the Oversight Committee's assessment.

President Obama intervened even as Holder was being held in contempt and—despite the president's assertion on Mexican television that neither he nor Holder knew anything about the whole affair—declared by executive privilege that the documents relating to Fast and Furious sought for so long by the Oversight Committee were finally off limits to the investigation, which is curious, given that the White House denied involvement in the program. Executive privilege is meant to protect communications between the president and his advisers and does not cover agencies' internal communications.

It is revealing that Obama and his team essentially tried every excuse they could think of to deny us the documents—while at the same time engaging in wholesale delays—before slamming the door shut altogether through an unusually expansive definition of executive-branch privilege. An awful lot of obfuscation for the "most transparent administration in history."

Two years later, DC District Judge Amy Berman Jackson, an Obama appointee, would find that the White House's assertion of executive privilege was far too broad. Finally, on the eve of the 2014 election, with practically the entire press and all of the political class thoroughly distracted, the DOJ would—after numerous defeats in the courts—release more than 64,000 pages of documents to us. They included emails that make one wonder whether Fast and Furious was part of a broad antigun strategy, not just a narrowly tailored anti–drug cartel strategy.

Included in the document dump was a personal favorite: an email from Eric Holder himself, which touched on guns—and me:

> Issa and his idiot cronies never gave a damn about this when all that was happening was that thousands of Mexicans were being killed with guns from our country. All they want to do—in reality—is cripple ATF [the Bureau of Alcohol, Tobacco, Firearms, and Explosives] and suck up to the gun lobby. Politics at its worst—maybe the media will get it.[1]

Well. Holder's email certainly reveals his disdain for me and for congressional oversight in general. But it is also telling about his motives for supporting Fast and Furious and suggests hostility to the Second Amendment. The criminally tragic irony is that the very operation Holder defended facilitated the death of hundreds of Mexican citizens, Brian Terry, and many others we may never know about.

Robert Heyer is Brian Terry's cousin and also chairs the Brian Terry Foundation, dedicated to honoring fallen Border Patrol agents. Speaking to what I think was the quietest Oversight Committee room I was ever in, he described that what had made Brian's death so shocking to his family is that he had not died on a foreign battlefield; he had been killed while in the line of duty as a US Border Patrol agent on US soil.

Heyer is adamant that it is not standard procedure to let weapons or contraband disappear untraced during an investigation— let alone to encourage the buying and selling of them and then let them disappear. Not even drugs or counterfeit currency is supposed to wander from agents' supervision, and there should always be a retrieval plan. "All those protocols went out the window," he says. ATF agents who objected, he added, were warned that they might be assigned less prestigious details if they didn't play along.

ATF special agent John Dodson, the key whistle-blower about Fast and Furious, claims he asked one of his superiors even before Terry's death whether he was prepared to go to a Border Patrol agent's funeral if the gun walking led to that—and was told that sometimes sacrifices have to be made. Did Eric Holder believe that, too? He refused to tell us.

Heyer is particularly angry about the fact that the family of Brian Terry was not informed by ATF or DOJ directly about the strange circumstances surrounding Terry's death. Only via whistle-blowers such as Dodson, the investigations of the Oversight Committee, and the media did the family learn that guns from Fast and Furious had contributed to Terry's death. "It wasn't 'til after that we began understanding the magnitude . . . how egregious this operation was," he says, citing a "lack of justice and accountability."

He claims from his conversations with agents who were involved that "none of the agents on the ground could see how the operation was going to be successful."

Critics of the Oversight Committee and of my chairmanship have tried to depict some of the investigations we have conducted, including Fast and Furious, as trumped-up political theater. That doesn't really bother me. It's the price one pays for being in the political line of fire. What I find unforgiveable is that many politicians and federal bureaucrats sought to thwart an Oversight Committee that was willing to rock the boat and dig for information outside the staid setting of a congressional hearing and provide the truth that the American people want—and that families of the dead like Brian Terry deserve.

These are not just wrangles over budgets or bureaucratic turf—not when lives are at stake. Without the efforts of the committee and the ATF whistle-blowers who aided us, Brian Terry's family might never have known the strong connection of the Fast and Furious program to the guns that killed him. Aside from the eventual contempt vote against Holder, far too few people were ever held accountable—a failing that must be laid directly at the feet of President Obama.

In the end, the cover-up didn't work, Eric Holder's reputation is forever tarnished, Fast and Furious utterly failed, and a good man with a full future had his life snuffed out because of it. Getting at those truths was neither easy nor pleasant. But it was necessary in order for the American people to know what their government had done and for a grieving family to gain some peace of mind.

That is why we made certain that the family of Brian Terry got their chance to address our full committee. We needed everyone to hear it, as told by Robert Heyer:

Brian was due to complete his shift of duty that night in the desert outside of Rio Pico at midnight on December 15 and then take some much deserved time off. He had already made his travel plans to fly back to Michigan and spend the Christmas holiday with his family. Brian's attention to detail had insured that all the Christmas gifts he had meticulously selected for his family had already been bought and sent in the mail prior to his arrival. Brian did ultimately come home that Christmas; we buried him not far from the house that he was raised in just prior to Christmas day. The gifts that Brian had picked out with such thought and care began to arrive in the mail that same week.

CHAPTER NINE

The Difference Benghazi Makes

B enghazi.

This midsized Libyan city four hundred miles from the capital, Tripoli, has evoked powerful emotions, public debates, and several congressional investigations that continue as of this writing. Add to it a major motion picture about the controversy such as *13 Hours*, and the controversy will not dissipate anytime soon—if ever. I certainly hope it doesn't.

What happened there on September 11, 2012, is at once hotly debated and frozen in time. And we are still grappling with fundamental questions: Were the attacks due to a dereliction of duty? Was it due to a careless security failure? Or utter confusion in the middle of the night? Was it an enigma that revealed itself slowly over weeks and months? Or a cover-up quickly coordinated to protect a president locked in a close reelection campaign?

To me, the answer is: all of the above. It is a case study in how a tragedy becomes a talking point and how a story becomes a lie.

I am enormously proud of the work that we on the Oversight Committee did to get the truth about the Benghazi attacks and to bring to the surface much of what the public now knows about them.

Some people did not like what we found out or the fact that we made it known. But I witnessed the anguish that some of our military felt about the misrepresentations of the commander in chief and his secretary of state. We saw also how official and political Washington enabled White House damage control.

In the end we uncovered fundamental truths about the attacks. That could not have been done in any way without the help of brave witnesses who came forward—often at great personal and professional risk—and insisted that the truth be told.

Of all the investigations that we undertook and of all the oversight hearings that we held exposing common mistakes and unprecedented corruption in government, what happened in Benghazi—and after—endures as perhaps the most disturbing. I cannot think of a circumstance we investigated that simultaneously revealed unparalleled valor in battle and the worst aspects of political war.

So much about the Benghazi attacks is part of the public record, yet some of the truth and most of the accountability have proven elusive. I will only tell here what we came to know, what we discovered to be true, and some that has yet to be told before.

The news of the attacks on September 11, 2012, came as a terrible shock. A US ambassador was dead—the first to be killed since 1979. Our consulate in Benghazi and a nearby annex that housed other American personnel were decimated by a massive, coordinated, multiwave assault that lasted several hours and included hundreds of attackers. Three other Americans were killed as well, defending themselves and their friends, some of whom survived because of the dead men's bravery under fire.

My heart was especially heavy when I heard that the murdered ambassador was Chris Stevens. I had met Chris many years earlier, and he was exactly the kind of person we need in our country's foreign service—energetic and idealistic, as well as practical and savvy. He cared deeply about the United States' standing in the world, and we could rely on him for a candid, honest assessment of conditions on the ground. Soon enough, we would find out just how honest he was.

Those of us on the Oversight Committee did not immediately assume that it was anything more than a terrible and deadly tragedy and that there were appropriate channels through which we would be able to determine what had happened and why. It was a large-scale attack—and the fact it happened on September 11 went a long way to establishing that it was a premeditated terrorist assault.

The White House was telling a different story: what had happened was a furious, spontaneous, mob-driven response to a YouTube video deemed offensive to Muslims. On September 14, White House Press Secretary Jay Carney said, "Let's be clear, these protests were in reaction to a video that had spread to the region."

A reporter then asked, "At Benghazi? What happened at Benghazi—"

Carney's reply: "We certainly don't know. We don't know otherwise. We have no information to suggest that it was a preplanned attack."[1]

We certainly did know otherwise. There was ample information it was a preplanned attack. Either Carney was lying, or he was repeating a lie. Then as now, the vast majority of our media have very much taken in stride being deceived by people in power. *That's all right, Jay. No hard feelings.*

That weekend, only five days after the attacks, UN Ambassador Susan Rice appeared on every major Sunday news program on network and cable television. A forceful personality and able television presence, she told and retold a form of this story:

"What happened in Benghazi was in fact initially a spontaneous reaction to what had just transpired hours before in
Cairo, almost a copycat of the demonstrations against our
facility in Cairo, prompted by the video.[2] . . . We do not—
we do not have information at present that leads us to conclude that this was premeditated or preplanned."[3]

At every appearance, she emphasized the video as the most critical cause. She stuck to her script and repeated it faithfully. What
she did was release a poisonous lie into the media and cultural
bloodstream. We are still dealing with the effects. What happened
in Benghazi was *not* spontaneous. What happened in Benghazi had
nothing to do with what had happened in Cairo. And the Obama
administration *absolutely* had information that it was premeditated
and preplanned.

These statements are not differences of opinion. They are not
conflicting recollections. They are not based on confusing recollections arising from the "fog of war."

President Obama made it known months later that he wished to
nominate Rice as his secretary of state, but he was forced to cancel
that plan once it became clear that she wouldn't be confirmed, even
by a Senate controlled by his fellow Democrats. Today she serves as
his national security advisor, a job appointment requiring only the
president's approval.

Rice's assertions—whether she knew they were false or not—
were a deliberate, desperate attempt to deflect blame, distract from
the truth, and ultimately dissuade Americans from placing blame for
the attack at the feet of the president as he was facing reelection—a
referendum on his presidency that was just two months away. Every
action by the Obama White House reinforces that conclusion.

Political people, when backed into a corner, resort to political means to avoid political damage.

Mission accomplished. For the remainder of the 2012 campaign, what had happened in Benghazi became yet another political back-and-forth in which many voters could hardly be blamed for not being able to determine which way was up. But many in our government were very much aware of what had happened, and just days after the deadly attack, they were coming to the Oversight Committee on their own with a much different story.

That is how we came to know—less than three weeks after the attacks—that it had been only the latest in a long line of assaults on Western diplomats in Libya in the months leading up to the Benghazi attacks. In fact, we learned of no fewer than thirteen separate security threats—and violent attacks—in the six months before September 11, 2012.

In one instance, on June 6, an explosive device blew a massive hole in a wall of the Benghazi compound that was described as "big enough for forty men to go through." Four days later, the car carrying the UK ambassador to Libya was attacked in an obvious assassination attempt. He escaped with his life, but a colleague in the car was killed. The pictures provided to us displayed shattered glass, twisted metal, and seats stained with blood, proving that it had been no random event.

At the same time, we found out something even more troubling: several government officials informed us that, prior to the attack, repeated requests had been made for increased security in Benghazi—some by Ambassador Stevens himself. All had been denied.

Learning that fact was important, but there was no joy in the discovery. For it meant that our most prominent leaders—including the president of the United States, the secretary of state, and the UN ambassador had not told the American people anything close to the truth. Instead, all three had provided false and misleading information that absolved themselves of blame and left the victims' families in the dark.

Reporter Sharyl Attkisson recounted her own first glimpse of Benghazi's secrets in the form of the unexpected approach of a US Special Forces officer who walked up to her one night in Virginia and said abruptly, "We were ready."

In her terrific book *Stonewalled*, Attkisson reported that she had been approached several times since the start of the Benghazi scandal by US personnel frustrated by their inability to make a difference during the attack—and angered by the administration's "spin" that made it professionally dangerous for them to tell their side of the story. My committee's job was to make it just a bit easier for them to tell the truth.

Less than a month after the Benghazi attack, the Oversight Committee held its first hearing. I felt we had to move fast and work together to investigate the issue and make sure that what we learned came to light and what we did not know could be unearthed as well. What we already knew was devastating.

The hearing took place on October 10, 2012. One day before, the State Department had begun coming clean about what occurred in Benghazi. It made two witnesses available for interviews and publicly acknowledged the truth that many had long suspected: there had been no protest in Cairo, and the attack had had nothing to do with a video made in California.

It quickly turned out that those revelations—as damaging as they were—were not all the State Department and Obama administration had known or concealed from the American people.

For example, the four individuals who told the story that became *13 Hours* we knew were out there—but we were denied access to them and several others who could have revealed what had really happened.

Four Who Were There

Four witnesses in particular put the lie to the Obama administration's story:

Eric Nordstrom, Regional Security Officer, Tripoli, Libya

At the first hearing, Nordstrom testified that on two separate occasions—in March and July 2012—he wrote to the State Department requesting an increase in the the US security presence in Benghazi. He never heard back. In fact, from December 2011 through July 2012, when he left Libya, no more than three Diplomatic Security Service agents were stationed at the Benghazi compound at any one time. Nordstrom told us he had requested that "at least five" personnel be stationed at Benghazi, but the State Department would not go along with his request.

In a tragic tone, he added, "It was abundantly clear that we were not going to get resources until the aftermath of an incident."

This is important because it explains the perilous security status of our facility, the fact that people on the ground such as Nordstrom had raised questions about it, and the fact that they had been turned down by their superiors at the State Department. We will never know if listening to people such as Nordstrom could have prevented the attack. What we do know is that it is part of the pattern: it was covered up and lied about, and it took a long time to get to the truth.

Gregory Hicks, State Department's Deputy Chief of Mission for Libya

On May 8, 2013, Gregory Hicks testified before our committee that for US staff in Tripoli, the evening of September 11, 2012, seemed to be ending in a peaceful fashion: no protests, no enraged mob, no rage toward YouTube. Hicks missed several calls from Ambassador Stevens. He called back shortly before 10 p.m. local time (4 p.m. in Washington, DC). "I got the ambassador on the other end, and he said, 'Greg, we're under attack.'"

Congressional hearings can be dull, but those words sent a chill throughout the entire room. *Greg, we're under attack.*

Soon after, Chris Stevens would be dead. Once Hicks told us what Stevens had told him, we understood a core truth about Benghazi. Hicks then added, "I was talking to the government of Libya, reporting to the State Department through the operations center, and also staying in touch with the Annex chief about what was going on."

During the night, Hicks was in touch with others as well. "Secretary Clinton called me and, along with her senior staff, were all on the phone. And she asked me what was going on. And I briefed her on developments."

I briefed her on developments.

That is important because it explains the truth about what the Obama administration knew, what Hillary Clinton knew, and when they knew it. Hicks was no doubt one of the last people to speak to Ambassador Stevens before he was killed. Those haunting last words—*Greg, we're under attack*—were dishonored by the absurd and destructive campaign to blame the attacks on a video.

Lieutenant Colonel Andrew Wood, Libya Site
Security Team Commander, 2012

The US Army Special Forces has a creed that is memorized and represented by every one of its members. Among its vows is: "I serve with the memory of those who have gone before me. I pledge to uphold the honor and integrity of their legacy in all that I am—in all that I do."

Lieutenant Colonel Andrew Wood has more than twenty-five years of experience as a Special Forces soldier. He knows the creed as well as anyone. He contacted our committee on his own and volunteered to tell the truth. I believe his motivation can be found in that soldier's creed. He knew we were being told stories that were not true.

Wood testified that he had first arrived in Libya in February 2012. While leading an elite Special Forces counterterrorism team consisting of sixteen men, he observed chaos, violence, battling militias, criminal activity, and increasing danger. He met every day with Chris Stevens, and the subject of security was a frequent topic of discussion.

In an interview with Sharyl Attkisson shortly before his testimony to the committee, Wood said that Stevens "was constantly concerned about the threats to not just himself but the entire staff there." Attkisson reported what we would later hear directly from witnesses—and once more, she had a news story all to herself. The rest of the mainstream media took little interest in the fact that during the six months leading up to the attack, Wood, Stevens, and staff made the case—over and over again—for tightened security in emails and diplomatic cables.

Wood also testified that there was an obvious and continuous reduction of US security personnel to protect Americans in Libya. "Shortly after I arrived, there was pressure to reduce the number of security people there." One by one, three State Department security teams were pulled out, and their only airplane, an upgraded DC-3 equipped to carry up to thirty-eight people, more than enough to evacuate all US personnel from Benghazi, was also taken away. Eventually, Wood's squad was removed as well. When Wood pressed for a change, the State Department told him to stop asking for help. And there was another message conveyed to him: "Don't even ask for Department of Defense support."

Like a good soldier, Lieutenant Colonel Wood followed orders and respected the chain of command. But by telling the truth, he also captured another part of the Special Forces creed: "I will not fail those in need. I will not bring shame upon myself or Special Forces."

Brigadier General Robert W. Lovell, US Air Force, Deputy Director for Intelligence, US African Command 2012

"We didn't know how long this would last when we became aware of the distress, nor did we completely understand what we had in front of us, be it a kidnapping, rescue, recovery, protracted hostile engagement, or any or all of the above. But what we did know quite early on was that this was a hostile action. This was no demonstration gone terribly awry."

Those are the words Gen. Lovell shared with us on May 1, 2014. He is another person with vital knowledge of what happened in Benghazi. He suffered in silence for the better part of eighteen months, knowing that the facts of that night were being obscured. So he came forward, and he shattered the White House's final myth about Benghazi.

What Lovell shared and what we now know is that there were no extraordinary efforts made to respond militarily to the Benghazi attacks that night. No jets or fighters or personnel were scrambled and put into motion in northern Italy (where the nearest US air base is located). No special assets were sent to the area as soon as it was known there was an attack. The excuse for that has been a dismissive response that there was no way to save the men who died at Benghazi and it was too late and too far for jets to reach the compound. And perhaps it was.

But Lovell's testimony was emphatic: "There are accounts of time, space, and capability discussions of the question: could we have gotten there in time to make a difference? Well, the discussion is not in the 'could or could not' in relation to time, space, and capability. The point is we should have tried."

The general then concluded, "As a saying goes: always move to the sound of the guns." Once the sound of guns in Benghazi was heard, the State Department and the Obama administration stood fast, rather than moving as fast as they could. To this day, they vehemently dispute any assertion that there was a "stand down" order. General Lovell made clear, however, that there was never a *go* order, either.

This is not an assertion that anyone in the State Department, the White House, or anywhere in our government "let our people die." Though we do not know if our people in Benghazi *could* have been saved, no military efforts of the kind General Lovell would have wanted *were* made.

Politicos, pundits, and even some of my colleagues in Congress have attempted to draw the nation into a picayune argument over whether any US forces were formally given an order to "stand down" rather than attempt to save the beleaguered personnel in Benghazi.

Some who were there say yes. Some in the intelligence community say no. But whether anyone ever said "stand down" or not, we know this: they stood down.

On September 11, 2012, as they faced repeated hostile attacks at a remote outpost, our fellow Americans in Libya were on their own. It's an abandonment that should never be forgiven.

Ready for Hillary–to Accept Responsibility

More than anyone else, Hillary Clinton will go down in history as playing a commanding role in Benghazi. Having demanded so much credit for our policies in Libya, she will always be singularly attached to their greatest failure. There's something very appropriate about that.

When questioned at a 2013 Senate hearing about the Benghazi attacks and how and why the American people had been misled by the Obama administration, Clinton shouted rhetorically, "What difference, at this point, does it make?" Interesting question; much of the Congress and country are still trying to answer it.

Hillary Clinton was an enthusiastic architect of both the decision to plunge the United States into the Libyan civil war and the campaign of deceit when the reckless policy produced deadly results in Benghazi. She was also among the most committed and enthusiastic promoters of the lie that the attacks were caused by the YouTube video. She directly referenced it on the night of the attacks, the next day, and the day after that.

Charles Woods, the father of Tyrone Woods, says he will never forget meeting Clinton on September 14, 2002, at a brief memorial service, as four flag-draped coffins carrying his son and our other three dead were brought home. At that somber and heartbreaking event, Woods related that Clinton approached him and said, "We are going to have the filmmaker arrested who was responsible for the death of your son."

That story always troubled me—its odd guarantee of the arrest of someone on the other side of the country, the weirdly specific assurance to a father steps away from his son's casket. It's bad enough to spin for the cameras to win the news cycle. What was to be gained by lying in private to one more person? Especially a grieving parent? I'd like to see even one member of the supposedly story-hungry mainstream media ask her about that.

On October 22, 2015, the House Select Committee on Benghazi heard more than eleven hours of testimony from Hillary Clinton. She was careful to control her temper and prevent further outbursts about what matters and what doesn't. But a bombshell still went off.

By that time, the revelations that Clinton had never used an official government email address and had even set up a private server in her own home had come to light. It has become clear to the entire country why she went to extraordinary lengths to communicate in secret and prevent any access to her emails: they contain a lot of truth about a lot of her lies.

On the night of the Benghazi attacks, Clinton emailed her daughter that "two of our officers were killed in Benghazi by an al Qaeda-like group."

The next afternoon, Clinton spoke with the Egyptian prime minister, and the notes taken by her staff about what she said (revealed only in October 2015) are devastating: "We know that the attack in Libya had nothing to do with the film. It was a planned attack—not a protest."

For days afterward, Clinton, Susan Rice, and president Obama focused like a laser on the video. But Clinton knew all along that it hadn't been the cause.

Hillary Clinton is now asking voters to make her the United States' commander in chief. But after her actions before, during, and after Benghazi, it's a job promotion she definitely does not deserve.

To me, the entire Benghazi investigation illustrates very well what many call the "80/20" rule. This means that one can often find 80 percent of the story by expending 20 percent of the effort—but discovering the last 20 percent of the truth requires the other 80 percent. We found out much of the story quickly: Benghazi was an enormously dangerous, unstable place. Requests for increased security were made and turned down. The attack was always known not to have been about a video. And no military assets had been scrambled or deployed to save our people who were under attack.

What we have come to know since is the sheer size of the Obama administration's cover-up and the dimension of the lies told to the American people.

It may seem ironic, but there is a YouTube video that I believe can help us understand the dimension of the failures of Benghazi and why, to this day, the wounds of the White House lies remain unhealed. The video to be watched captures another tragic day: February 1, 2003. It is a live transmission of NASA Mission Control in Houston as the space shuttle *Columbia* is making its final reentry to Earth and is mere minutes from landing safely back home. Without warning, the unthinkable happens: systems begin to fail, contact with the astronauts is cut off, and within moments, *Columbia* disintegrates before one's eyes. All seven members of the crew—who NASA was tasked with bringing home safely—are dead.

As the terrible events unfold, Flight Director Leroy Cain is seen looking concerned, then stunned, and eventually lost in grief. But then he does something remarkable: he stands up and commands, "Lock the doors." That was not to keep the outside world from learning what had happened; it was the first step of preserving information, securing everything they knew and everything they would learn.

He then begins a checklist for his colleagues—all of them thunderstruck by what has just happened—issuing numerous instructions to preserve documents, files, tapes—everything. He says, "No phone calls outside this room. No data transmissions into or out."

Cain knows that Columbia has been destroyed. He knows that the flight crew has died a horrible death. He knows that a painstakingly detailed investigation will be undertaken. He knows that the truth will be determined, responsibility must be taken, and careers—especially his—will be affected forever. But he does not hesitate.

This is what accountability looks like.

What a shame that on the night of September 11, 2012, the Obama White House and Secretary of State Hillary Clinton—confronted with another kind of shocking development and the terrible death of colleagues—acted differently. They also locked the doors, but it wasn't to begin a public process to determine the truth; it was to launch a private campaign to create a false narrative, to explain it away for a while and cover up what they knew so the facts wouldn't come out.

Within months, an exhaustive and transparent investigation made public every detail of every mechanical failure of the shuttle and every human mistake at NASA that had contributed to the destruction of the ship and claimed the lives of its crew.

We are to this day still dragging the truth out of the Obama administration, unearthing more information that Hillary Clinton knew but didn't share, and fighting the forces that see only the political damage it may cause and resist doing so at any cost.

It was all so unnecessary. Telling the truth about its mistakes and miscalculations would not have affected the White House nearly as seriously as has the exposure of its appalling attempts to explain it all away and avoid answering for anything. The folks in the White House couldn't handle the truth, so they relentlessly advanced a lie.

So let's answer Clinton's question: What difference, at this point, does it make?

Benghazi makes a difference, because the truth makes a difference. By refusing to let this tragedy get swept aside and forgotten, we are honoring Chris Stevens, Glen Doherty, Sean Smith, and Tyrone Woods. They deserved better from a government that was duty-bound to protect them. Their families and their fellow citizens deserved the truth about how and why they had died, not fabrications created to serve White House damage control.

Benghazi may not have changed our nation in 2012 as it might have, or even should have. But thanks to the testimony we heard, the facts that were brought to light and the emotion of a movie such as *13 Hours*, I believe we must all now confront what happened that night and work to put an end to the waiting for the families, friends, and survivors who know that the full truth has yet to be told.

President Obama and Hillary Clinton should have long ago come clean and made this right. Is there anyone left to lie to?

CHAPTER TEN

Lois Lerner: The Power to Tax and the Power to Destroy

You don't need to be a conservative to endorse the well-known axiom "The power to tax involves the power to destroy." It's an observation attributed to two men involved in one case before the US Supreme Court in 1819: Daniel Webster, the great statesman and eminent US senator, and John Marshall, perhaps the most influential of all chief justices of the Court.

Though Senator Webster and Chief Justice Marshall could not have conceived of the Internal Revenue Service and never met Lois Lerner (the former director of the IRS Exempt Organizations unit), I have a feeling they knew her kind very well. They warned against just such an abuse of power. But to this day, the serial misconduct and appalling scandal surrounding the Internal Revenue Service continue to anger so many Americans who know that its proper role is that of impartial tax collection.

The chain of events leading to officials of the IRS directly and systematically targeting Tea Party and conservative groups by denying approval of their nonprofit tax status can be traced to the Supreme Court's 2010 Citizens United decision.

That case redefined the funding of political messages by non-profits. The left portrayed the decision as opening the floodgates to donations to elections and also looked with great suspicion at the rise of grassroots Tea Party groups that opposed big government and President Obama. Surely the administration realized that organized groups with Tea Party principles could translate into highly motivated Republican voters come November 2012.

Ever since then, to the liberal left and much of the media, Citizens United has stood as a sort of original sin of the Supreme Court, falsely blamed for any number of real or imagined problems with the United States' campaigns and elections. The president inspired many Democratic activists and, it appears, more than a few people in the federal bureaucracy to treat combating the new wave of conservative applicants as an urgent duty. Many legislators saw it that way as well. Senator Jeff Merkley (D-OR) warned that we needed to be on the lookout for "a shadowy front group," while Senator Charles Schumer (D-NY) warned, "The public is under siege from shadowy special interest groups."

At the IRS itself, some employees appear to have reacted enthusiastically to the uproar, demanding strict scrutiny of conservative groups. Lois Lerner advised her IRS colleagues that they should "do a c4 project next year" focusing on existing organizations. She even showed her recognition that such an effort would approach dangerous ground and could not be perceived as a "per se political project." Quick rule of Washington: when people say they're doing a project that is not "per se political"—it's political.

In a speech at Duke University the month prior to the 2010 election, Lerner admitted the political pressure being brought to bear on the IRS: "They want the IRS to fix the problem . . . everybody is screaming at us right now: 'Fix it now before the election. Can't you see how much these people are spending?' . . . I can't do anything right now."[1]

Answering the call to arms in early 2011, Lerner directed the manager of an IRS Technical Unit to subject Tea Party cases to a "multi-tier review," and characterized Tea Party cases as "very dangerous."[2] That is why it cannot be disputed that after Citizens United, the IRS began systematically targeting new Tea Party groups for extra scrutiny and delaying (sometimes for years) their applications for nonprofit tax status. That began shortly after the midterm elections of 2010, which saw Republicans—driven by Tea Party activism—retaking control of the House and ending the Democrats' absolute control over Congress. Republicans have been in the majority ever since.

By early 2012, Tea Party groups and conservatives began to complain about delays at the IRS. Representative Jim Jordan (R-OH) was hearing about such incidents firsthand, and he brought them to many people's attention. Could it be that the IRS was granting or denying nonprofit applications based upon the name of an organization, if it spelled out its political leanings?

Upon first hearing the claims, few were convinced that the worst was true. Though underhanded maneuvering and even dirty tricks will always happen in politics, it was difficult to believe that the IRS would single out and act against law-abiding Americans strictly because of their political beliefs. Still, the Oversight Committee staff performed its due diligence and even met with IRS officials to inquire into the allegations and make sure there was an appropriate explanation. One IRS director, Lois Lerner, downplayed the rumors and denied everything—even the hint of wrong-doing.

It was hardly a convincing performance, so Jim Jordan and I took the lead in requesting the Treasury Inspector General for Tax Administration (TIGTA) to follow up. In truth, we expected a fairly quick turnaround and for not much more than routine information to come back. But as the months went by, we began to wonder what was happening. And the IG was not being communicative. Maybe it was onto something? That went on for more than a year.

But in May 2013, at a relatively obscure tax conference in Washington, DC, sponsored by the American Bar Association, Lerner detailed—for the first time—how the IRS division she headed had indeed looked more skeptically at applications that "used names like Tea Party or Patriots." And she specifically stated that IRS "line people in Cincinnati" had been at fault.[3]

We know now that Lerner's revelation came in advance of the public release of an audit report from TIGTA confirming that the IRS had used "inappropriate criteria" to target Tea Party and other conservative political groups. This is what is known as trying to get ahead of the story—but Lerner's alarming revelation immediately drew attention, and scrutiny.

After hearing the news of the day, a well-known politician said, "Americans are right to be angry about it, and I am angry about it." His name was Barack Obama. He further added, "Our administration has to make sure that we are working hand in hand with Congress to get this thing fixed."[4] Hand in hand? More like with a raised fist and bent elbow. What should have been a thorough search for what had happened, why it had happened, and who had been responsible was instead obstructed by an executive-branch commitment to delay, deny, deceive, and, as we later found out, destroy.

Our investigation did yield extraordinary results and revealed one of the most serious acts of wrongdoing seen in any investigation we undertook—one of the worst seen in Washington in many decades. The investigation was also one of the most disappointing in terms of a joint search for the truth. As we discovered the facts, verified their accuracy, and brought them to the public, we did so without any cooperation from the White House. In fact, it fought us all the way.

On the committee, my Democratic colleagues pivoted almost instantaneously from showing concern to muddying the investigatory waters, attacking the messengers, and misleading the American people. That never stopped and continues to this day, which reflects poorly on them. No matter what your party or politics may be, we all have a stake in stopping abuses by the IRS. My Democratic colleagues should have done better.

Though the Democrats' tactics made our work more difficult and denied the public some of what it deserves to know, what we came to learn was this: Lois Lerner is a political partisan who expressed a personal dislike of conservatives and who abused her authority in order to limit the political participation of Americans whose beliefs she did not agree with.

She lied about the Cincinnati office; the targeting was orchestrated out of IRS headquarters in Washington. She lied about the intentional targeting of Tea Party groups; there was a "be on the look out" document designed to highlight conservative groups for greater scrutiny. She also lied about her involvement in the targeting and not attempting to cover up what she and those who worked for her did.

In one email, she directly warned a colleague about congressional oversight: "I was cautioning folks about email and how we have had several occasions where Congress has asked for emails and there has been an electronic search for responsive emails—so we need to be cautious about what we say in emails." In the same conversation, she then asked whether OCS conversations were searchable. Upon learning they were not, she responded, "Perfect."[5]

Perfect? Why would it be perfect for no electronic record of her communications to be maintained?

That was only one of the many questions Lois Lerner could have answered and only one of the clarifications she could have provided when she was called to testify before the Oversight Committee on May 22, 2013. It was a memorable morning, to say the least. After reading an opening statement asserting her innocence and claiming she had done nothing improper, she then refused to testify by pleading the Fifth Amendment so as not to incriminate herself.

Though it's far from unprecedented for witnesses to claim the privilege, it's generally not done *after* reading a statement professing complete innocence—essentially forcing your claim into the public record (and every news program) and then refusing to answer questions you don't want to answer. My committee colleague and former federal prosecutor, Representative Trey Gowdy (R-SC), immediately objected and later added that he had noted seventeen separate assertions made by Lerner about the case, each of them invalidating her claim to Fifth Amendment protection.

In any US courtroom, Lerner's gambit—daring as it was—would never be tolerated. But Congress has few tools to compel a witness to testify. It can hold a witness in contempt but has to refer the matter to the US attorney for the District of Columbia for enforcement, which seemed all but impossible with Eric Holder at the helm of the Justice Department.

Denied Lerner's testimony, we undertook to do the job of getting to the bottom of the scandal and figuring out what had happened and why.

After examining more than a million IRS, Treasury Department, and DOJ documents and conducting more than fifty interviews with officials from all three offices, we determined that conservative groups had been intentionally and consistently targeted. Between February 2010 (the first full month after the Citizens United decision) and May 2013 (when Lerner admitted having given Tea Party groups more scrutiny), not a single Tea Party group had its application for nonprofit status approved. Not one.

For more than two years, from early 2010 through mid-2012, the IRS flagged nonprofit applicants using terms such as "Tea Party," "Patriots," and "9/12," observing whether the groups using them were "good" nonprofits or used "emotional" propaganda with "little educational value."

Groups' donors and core beliefs were scrutinized. Jenny Beth Martin from Tea Party Patriots told the Oversight Committee in January 2014 that her group had experienced a three-year delay in processing and intrusive questioning. Disturbingly, the tactics seem to have worked, as the suppression of Tea Party activities during the crucial 2012 elections was an obvious side effect.

Claims that conservative and Tea Party applicants were simply victims of careless mistakes or poor customer service were proven false by the fact that when presented with one very politically connected tax-exempt applicant, the IRS handled the matter quite differently.

In 2011, the Barack H. Obama Foundation, which was founded and operated by the president's half brother Abon'go Malik Obama, applied to the IRS for tax-exempt status. At the same time as numerous Tea Party and conservative organizations were facing years of delays and denials, the IRS approved the Obama Foundation's request in only thirty-four days. The IRS helpfully also agreed to give the group retroactive status back to 2009, when it had started its fund-raising.

Lois Lerner signed the paperwork personally. Now, that's customer service.

Though Lerner represented herself as a diligent, meticulous thirty-four-year career civil servant, she was, in truth, a very well compensated government professional. Curiously, the IRS gave her large bonuses at exactly the time the application delays were occurring. From 2010 to 2013, she was awarded a total of $129,300 in bonus compensation, which stopped in November 2012, when the IRS informed Lerner she had exceeded the $230,700 per calendar year salary limit on federal employees.

That's right: the Obama administration thought so highly of the performance of Lois Lerner that it made her one of the highest paid federal employees in America. Might Lois Lerner have gotten her marching orders from the White House when she deviated from the purely nonpartisan role IRS evaluators were supposed to play? Did someone in the Obama administration echo what Henry II is said to have raged about Thomas Becket: "Will no one rid me of this troublesome Tea Party?" Or did she merely answer President Obama's call to action from the bully pulpit?

It was not the earliest instance in which Lerner acted in a biased fashion just when Democrats needed it, either. We learned that at least one colleague from her time at the Federal Election Commission (FEC) in the late 1980s and '90s says she showed extra suspicion of conservative groups around the time of the pivotal 1994 congressional elections, in which the Republicans retook both houses of Congress. In fact, she had been called to testify before the Oversight Committee at the time, responding to charges of biased enforcement at the FEC. Nearly two decades later, opportunity and circumstance collided: as head of the Exempt Organizations unit at the IRS, the deeply biased Lerner was in exactly the right place, at exactly the right time, to respond to Obama's plea for action on Citizens United.

Not surprisingly, Attorney General Holder played his part in the cover-up, or at least in what appeared to be one, appointing as lead investigator into the matter a substantial donor to past Obama campaigns. The DOJ's Public Integrity Section and the FBI also looked into the IRS's targeting of conservatives—but were surely tainted by having met with Lerner in 2010 to discuss possible criminal charges *against the conservative groups* at the behest of Democrat senators.

In 2014, as she remained uncooperative about her lost emails and refused to tell the truth to our committee and the American people, I introduced a resolution holding Lois Lerner in contempt of Congress. The House of Representatives approved the contempt citation on May 7, 2014. To no one's surprise, Holder's Department of Justice refused to move forward. But though this thwarted legal accountability, it did nothing to stop the disturbing truth from coming to light and merely reinforced the emerging public notion that the IRS—and by extension the Obama administration—had a great deal to hide.

In response, Democrats advanced the claim that "line workers" in the Cincinnati IRS office had been to blame—due to "confusion" over the law, an overwhelming caseload, or perhaps something more sinister. So our investigators interviewed IRS employees there and got the truth, which came pouring out of the workers: they had simply been following direction from Lerner and others at IRS headquarters in Washington. They apparently had little interest in being the scapegoats.

As that excuse was being demolished, congressional Democrats made misleading claims about the targeting. Several Democrats, including Ranking Member Elijah Cummings, Ranking Member Sander Levin (D-MI), and Representative Gerry Connolly (D-VA), falsely asserted that the IRS had targeted liberal-oriented groups, based on documents selectively produced and selectively released by the IRS.

Our team diligently got to the bottom of that spin, determining that only seven applications in the IRS backlog contained the word "progressive" and that every one had eventually been approved. Tea Party groups were subjected to unprecedented review and experienced years-long delays. Other IRS employees would later testify that the level of scrutiny Lerner ordered for the Tea Party cases was unprecedented.

It was enough to make us think that the IRS really couldn't be trusted.

Mention of two dutiful public servants needs to be made: the resolute IRS inspector general, Russell George, and his deputy, Timothy Camus. During the investigation, they endured escalating personal attacks by Cummings and other Democrats, culminating in an outrageous call for an ethics investigation against them, an effort to dirty them or convince them to back down. But both George and Camus were intrepid in their work and repeatedly pierced false narratives by the agency and even the IRS commissioner himself. They deserve our appreciation for their honest efforts, not the scorn heaped on them by Democrats in what was an especially low moment.

As he did in so many of our investigations, in 2013, Cummings—shortly after our work began—abruptly declared, "The case is solved" on a Sunday news show. He quickly retreated from that significant inaccuracy, returning to the safety of the usual fierce attacks on me, with which he always seemed most comfortable. But how better to know if you're onto something than experiencing others attacking you personally instead of substantively?

One of the most troubling aspects of the entire investigation was attempting to fulfill our proper and routine requests for Lois Lerner's emails. They would seem to have been of intense interest to an innocent person, for if they showed no evidence of anything, Lerner could fairly have said she was exonerated. But as with so much of the scandal, the more we looked, the more we found troubling evidence of a cover-up.

The IRS first insisted that it had simply "lost" two years of emails belonging to Lerner, from January 2009 through April 2011, which is an extraordinary coincidence since that is the precise period of time when Tea Party groups were being targeted and denied nonprofit status. According to the government watchdog group Judicial Watch, the IRS further said that a computer crash had claimed all recoverable records of Lerner emails to the White House, Democratic members of Congress, the Treasury Department, and the Department of Justice.

Over the course of the investigations into the scandal, IRS Commissioner John Koskinen repeatedly assured our committee that he would provide all of Lois Lerner's emails and every available data source would be searched, including her computer hard drive, her BlackBerry, email backup tapes, the backup tapes for the server drives, and then, finally, the loaner laptop computers.

It didn't happen.

IRS Deputy Inspector General Timothy Camus testified that IRS employees only cursorily checked her hard drive; it appears that more could have been done to recover data from that source. Instead, all data were deemed unrecoverable after a brief search. Camus said, "We're not aware that they searched any one in particular. They did— it appears they did look into initially whether or not the hard drive had been destroyed, but they didn't go much further than that."[6]

That helps explain why Camus also told the Oversight Committee, "There is potential criminal activity" at the IRS. The failed non-search for Lerner's emails meant that a thousand emails were not found until Camus's office itself searched backup tapes—because the IRS never looked for them in the first place: "To the best we can determine through the investigation, *they just simply didn't look for those e-mails*."[7]

Because of actions undertaken by the IRS, 24,000 of Lois Lerner's emails were "accidentally" lost, along with her computer hard drive, which the agency also destroyed. Commissioner Koskinen stated that the IRS had made "extraordinary efforts" to recover any emails, but that is simply not credible. John Koskinen is a highly accomplished individual, and he has done his reputation great harm by trafficking in false assurances, clumsy cover-ups, and, yes, obvious lies. Of all the agencies of the federal government, the IRS is the last place anybody would believe would fall victim to an inability to track down records and then perform a passive, slipshod search for information if it truly wants to find it. By late October 2015, the

House would be considering impeachment proceedings against Koskinen.

And so it went. An excuse for the IRS was advanced, and our team had to open an investigation, discover the facts, compile a report, and present the facts to the world. It was painstaking and time-consuming—but punching holes in a cover-up always is. We expect partisan behavior from elected politicians. That's politics. From the most basic—and most powerful—executive-branch agencies, though, we must demand a commitment to impartiality and fundamental fairness—even when the political stakes are high.

It's a standard President Obama failed to live up to. Though it is true that he managed to display a degree of displeasure for what Lerner initially admitted had occurred, he then made a very calculated effort not to repeat even his gentle condemnation of Lerner or her office. In May 2013, he had claimed to be "angry." Nine months later, his rage had not only somewhat subsided but had gone away entirely, and he said the investigation into the activities of the IRS had proved "not even a smidgen of corruption."

Obama may think that is the equivalent of holding the line against his critics, but it was a major missed opportunity to show that he realizes that the massive power of the IRS being wrongly directed against political activists of any stripe is repulsive. Deployed against conservative nonprofits precisely when it was, however, the IRS's effort had all the appearance of political strategizing aimed at helping the administration and the Democrat Party. That is why the attempts to cover up the affair, rather than letting sunlight in to act as a disinfectant, continue to damage President Obama, undermining his credibility in the eyes of everyone but his most loyal liberal supporters.

Since Watergate, it had often been remarked that "the cover-up is worse than the crime." Perhaps. But what we know now is that at the IRS, the cover-up and the crime were one and the same. The act of restricting the rights of Tea Party conservatives, the extensive efforts to conceal it from public view, and the many lies told in furtherance of both were a shocking abuse of power, all the more shameful because they constituted an attack on the central rights of our democracy.

One of Lerner's now infamous emails was a 2011 message to one of her colleagues: "No one will ever believe that both your hard drive and mine crashed within a week of each other! Life is strange." Like a bank robber safely speeding off in a getaway car, Lerner here mocked the truth, the law, and even Daniel Webster and Justice Marshall. She used her power to destroy, took gleeful satisfaction in the telling, and slunk off to a comfortable retirement with a six-figure pension from her years at the top of the federal pay scale. Not a bad career if your ambition is to thwart the rights of your fellow Americans.

Ultimately, she may get away with it.

In October 2015, the Justice Department announced that it would not prosecute Lerner, stating "Our investigation uncovered substantial evidence of mismanagement, poor judgment, and institutional inertia, leading to the belief by many tax-exempt applicants that the IRS targeted them based on their political viewpoints. But poor management is not a crime."[8]

Though poor management is not a crime, intentionally obstructing the constitutional rights of Americans is. If there are good or even defensible reasons not to prosecute Lerner, this argument is not even close to presenting them. In fact, the DOJ's statement drips with the same condescension of most every other cover-up associated with Obama administration scandals and IRS abuses. Calling it "institutional inertia" is neither a reasonable explanation nor even an accurate description. On the contrary, Lerner and her underlings demonstrated great energy and initiative. Their back-and-forth emails run into the thousands of pages and detail significant effort at all levels to run Tea Party and conservative groups through a never-ending process of examination and review. Those people were hard at work for years to accomplish that.

For the DOJ to state that IRS actions were "leading to the belief by many tax-exempt applicants that the IRS targeted them based on their political viewpoints" is a crude insult at odds with the plain facts. The IRS inspector general concluded that "Criteria for selecting applications inappropriately identified organizations based on their names and policy positions," that the IRS also "requested unnecessary information for many potential political cases," and that "potential political cases experienced long processing delays" much longer than similar cases.[9]

The decision to close the IRS targeting investigation without a single charge or prosecution is a low point of accountability for the Obama administration, which has proven to be far more interested in punishing whistle-blowers than in punishing the abuse and misconduct they expose. Confronted with misconduct, it has shielded those involved from responsibility. Giving Lois Lerner a free pass only reinforces the idea that government officials are above the law and that there are no consequences for wrongdoing.

"Lying to Congress is a felony," wrote Cleta Mitchell, a lawyer to Tea Party groups, in the *Wall Street Journal.* "But the Obama Justice Department has not lifted a finger to prosecute anyone responsible for the IRS scandal, including top brass who repeatedly gave false testimony to Congress. Neither has Congress done much about being lied to by the IRS."[10] Shameful but true.

That is why Americans' faith in government and the Obama administration has eroded. We already knew that the devastation to the credibility of the IRS would be decades in the repairing. Now the Department of Justice, the credibility of its US attorneys, and the independence of the inspectors general stand damaged as well.

CHAPTER ELEVEN

Hillary's Got a Secret (Email Server)

The email scandal that swamped Hillary Clinton in 2015 and threatened to derail her presidential candidacy in 2016 was actually years in the making. Like a raging fire that burns down an entire building, this ethical inferno began as a spark, spread unseen, and eventually helped engulf her reputation, her tenure in office, and her bid for the White House.

But this was no lightning strike near dry tinder. Mrs. Clinton did it all on her own. That is why the blame is falling solely on her shoulders. It has revealed all we need to know about her obsession with secrecy, her determination to circumvent the law, and her commitment to serial excuses to avoid being found out.

The spectrum of this Clinton scandal should be understood in three parts:

- As a shameful ethical failing
- As an obvious violation of the law
- And as a reckless disregard for the United States' national security

Though any one of these factors should disqualify Mrs. Clinton from holding higher office, the full measure of what she's done and what she is still doing cast great shame upon her and her colleagues and enablers, while also doing damage to our system of government transparency and public accountability.

Still, as serious as this is, we may owe Hillary Clinton a measure of gratitude. Nothing else in recent history illustrates more precisely what is wrong with Washington, what broke down in the Obama administration, and the stakes for stopping her from winning the White House.

Why Didn't Hillary Include Us in Her Email Address Book?

Here is what we know.

Upon entering office as our nation's sixty-seventh Secretary of State, Hillary Clinton declined the official government email address that is assigned to literally every single federal official in the world who serves this country. The practice is not simply a matter of convenience or even uniformity, but first and foremost a matter of facilitating secure communications among our officials, as well as with other vital contacts spanning the globe.

Why did she do this?

It is a hallmark of Washington's incurable obtuseness that we are still debating various aspects of this fundamental question when the sole and only answer is as plain as the private computer server that was in her home in Chappaqua, New York: she did not want any congressional scrutiny, public access, or historical record of the way she did business while secretary of state.

This goes far beyond what some have hastily interpreted as a Clintonian "penchant for secrecy." We should be so lucky!

What her private email network did was create a back-channel so Clinton could communicate with her shadowy network of advisers *so even the Obama White House would not know.*

We know that this allowed her to seek and receive advice from confidants such as Sidney Blumenthal, a onetime journalist who at the time was seeking to do business deals around the world while receiving a six-figure annual consulting contract from the Clinton Foundation. Mrs. Clinton had sought to add Blumenthal to her official team at the State Department, only to be explicitly prohibited by the Obama administration from hiring him.

This was no complicated desire on her part to create a safe place for her to exchange candid emails with friends, family, and colleagues past and present. It was a move of naked intent to fully or partially shield her communications from court orders or congressional subpoenas, as well as Freedom of Information Act requests that bind citizens—no matter how powerful—and empower citizens—no matter how ordinary.

There is, quite simply, no other explanation.

In fact, her longtime political confidant, the saurian campaign consultant James Carville, committed a classic gaffe by uttering an entirely truthful statement when asked why she had done it: "I suspect she didn't want Louie Gohmert rifling through her e-mails."

That would be Congressman Louie Gohmert of Texas, an attorney who served in the US Army's Judge Advocate General's Corps, as a Texas district judge, and also as chief justice of the state's 12th District Court of Appeals. How revealing that one of Hillary's closest friends would name Representative Gohmert as the kind of person she would be most afraid of seeing her emails while serving as secretary of state.

But in that sense, Carville is right. Hillary refused to use the official email service because she wanted to communicate with her closest confidants (in and out of government) in secret. And she did so for patently obvious reasons: she knew that her communications would or could prove embarrassing to her personally, reveal her shady dealings, or even expose her to criminal liability.

Now we know it was all three.

We also know that she was enabled not only by her closest staff members in government (one of whom, Huma Abedin, was also given a personal email address on Mrs. Clinton's private server) but by a vast number of people who communicated with her by email—including President Obama, who exchanged at least eighteen emails with her.

How many of those people are, in actuality, enablers of what she did?

That President Obama is on record as claiming he learned of Clinton's email practices from media reports is, at this point, mostly unimportant. He has so many times claimed that he first learned of his administration's scandals from either reading the newspapers or watching television that his obvious dissembling carried no weight and did not mitigate the scandal.

What it did prove, however, is that the knowledge that Clinton was operating outside the law was not only kept quiet by her hand-picked coterie but was also known to individuals at the highest levels of our government and scores of people in between.

That is fundamentally why this ethical storm will remain right over Hillary's head, haunting her candidacy and further damaging her character. Even as you read this, she is searching for a workable excuse for what she did because the only material not available to her is the truth.

She tried ignoring the issue. That didn't work.

She tried downplaying it. It didn't go away.

She tried denying that she had sent or received any classified material on her private email system. Since then, every few days a new discovery has revealed the sheer scope of her lies: thousands of classified, confidential, and even top secret documents have been found in her emails. It is an insult to the intelligence of every American that Mrs. Clinton hangs on to her increasingly absurd story.

She tried saying "Everyone does it" by noting that some of her predecessors communicated a few times via personal email addresses (emails the government has always had in its possession). That excuse also failed because she built and employed a private server that captured *every* email she sent and stored it for her private review and, by her own admission, deletion of tens of thousands of her emails. None of her predecessors had done anything like that.

She tried making a joke when asked if she had wiped her server clean of emails: "You mean, like with a cloth"? I guess you had to be there.

No one even chuckled at the attempted humor because there's nothing funny about what Clinton did and it is no laughing matter that she has forced us to confront her insistence that what we know to be true is, instead, obviously false.

And it's more than a serious scandal; her tissue-thin denials also open a window into the way she thinks, her sense of entitlement, and her apparently unshakable belief that the normal rules don't apply to her.

Perhaps they do not. But the law sure should.

Will the Defendant Please Rise?
(That Means You, Mrs. Clinton)

Though it is beyond obvious that Hillary is in political trouble stemming from her conduct, she should be in serious legal jeopardy as well.

In recent years, our government has prosecuted to the letter of the law the mishandling of classified information, including the federal indictment of even David Petraeus, a four-star general, one of the United States' most respected military commanders, and, most, recently, the director of the Central Intelligence Agency.

Did Petraeus set up a private email server and collect, sift through, and destroy email communications so that no one else could read them? No.

Did he create a shady back-channel network of friends and former associates with potential financial interests in his work to whom he gave improper access? No.

Did he violate the law? Yes, he did. He improperly showed classified documents related to military issues to his biographer, a military intelligence reservist. No one has alleged that US security was ever compromised, but that is no excuse. This may seem a small issue to some, but it is attached to a very important principle. What Petraeus did was wrong, and I suspect he always knew that it was. He was made to suffer severe consequences as he pled guilty and had to resign from office.

Mrs. Clinton's connection to this issue is absolute.

If Hillary received or read a single email sent to her about the sacking of Petraeus or his being charged with a crime of mishandling classified material, it would have been handled by her private unsecured email server, on which were stored thousands of classified documents.

The *Washington Post* also reported that Mrs. Clinton was completely aware she was operating outside the rules:

> On Feb. 27, 2011, Clinton was forwarded an email from someone named John Godfrey, whom an aide described to Clinton as "one of our most knowledgeable officers on Libya." Godfrey's email included a lengthy analysis of a post-Gaddafi Libya, including a section that State Department reviewers withheld from public release due to their assessment that it includes classified information.
>
> Clinton responded, "Who does he work for now?" and close aide Jake Sullivan responded, "Us." Clinton ironically then replied with the following, showing a clear understanding that most State Department officials were expected to use their official government accounts to conduct public business: "I was surprised that he used a personal account if he is at State."[1]

For these reasons and others, I believe that Mrs. Clinton should be made to answer for her actions in a court of law. The federal law governing these rules (18 U.S. Code § 1924) is very clear and reads as follows:

> Whoever, being an officer, employee, contractor, or consultant of the United States, and, by virtue of his office, employment, position, or contract, becomes possessed of documents or materials containing classified information of the United States, knowingly removes such documents or materials without authority and with the intent to retain such documents or materials at an unauthorized location

shall be fined under this title or imprisoned for not more than one year, or both.

I am more than skeptical that she will be charged with this or any other crime, for the plain reason that it would have to be approved by the Justice Department and the current attorney general, Loretta Lynch, is a large political donor to Democratic candidates and President Obama's campaigns.

Whether Secretary Clinton becomes Defendant Clinton or not, I am certain of this much: she will never extricate herself from this scandal. The reason is that Americans must share the faith that we are all equal in the eyes of the law.

She may avoid formal federal prosecution, but tens of millions of Americans will decide for themselves—even if they might share her political leanings or at one time could have envisioned her sitting behind the desk of the Oval Office.

They will know that they themselves would never have been so lucky. They will conclude that Barack Obama's Justice Department would never give them an easy pass were they to do what she did. And they will realize that this obvious double standard is a failing that Hillary Clinton will have forced upon our system of law and order.

Safeguarding Her Secrets While Exposing America's

It may seem hard to believe, but Mrs. Clinton's wrongdoing may even go beyond her widespread ethical lapses and potential criminal mishandling of classified information. By utilizing a private network outside of secure government systems, she may have revealed everything she sent or received not only to troublemaking computer hackers in this country or even allies interested in eavesdropping on us, but to hostile entities around the world.

In fact, Robert Gates, who served as President Obama's first secretary of defense, has said, "I think the odds are pretty high" that Clinton's server was accessed by agents of Russia, China, and even Iran. Gates has also reveled that the Pentagon routinely has to fend off 100,000 cyberattacks on its computer systems *every day*, a full-scale breach of which is prevented only by its advanced encryption systems. Clinton's server could never have withstood anything of the sort.

Some emails have come to light that I am sure Mrs. Clinton would have preferred remain hidden: the fact that she hasn't driven a car in more than twenty years; asking an assistant to *call another assistant* to fetch her iced tea; and seeking tech support from her staff on how to find out when her favorite shows are on television. Perhaps requests like these are not all that uncommon among very privileged people removed from everyday life and in positions of great power.

When the existence of her server became public, is it possible she remembered this email to her daughter Chelsea Clinton, sent the night of the deadly attack on our compound in Benghazi, Libya? And how it contradicted her public statements that a YouTube video had been to blame? "Two of our officers were killed in Benghazi by an Al Qaeda-like group."

Or perhaps this transcript of her phone call the following day to the prime minister of Egypt, when she said, "We know the attack in Libya had nothing to do with the film. It was a planned attack, not a protest."

* * *

Apart from notes that show Mrs. Clinton to be at odds with the truth, there is also an enormous amount of daily email traffic that involves the secretary of state (widely termed America's "top diplomat") that would be of considerable interest to other nations, even if, as Secretary Clinton has falsely asserted, they contained no classified info. Those are the notes she should be far more embarrassed about coming to light.

Who the people she talked to are—or preferred not to have a dialogue with—is information that we want to keep in house. Other nations would just about do anything to find out which staff have most influence with Clinton, as well as the direct contacts she took from the White House, Congress, and elsewhere. How she made decisions and the words she used, in her own voice, would be a treasure trove to any foreign interest, whether it wished us well or ill.

Because her immediate network was likely targeted for surveillance, she exposed every single one of the people she communicated with to undue influence, pressure, and targeting.

Certainly an administration that was targeting the communications of our own allies, including leaders such as Germany's prime minister, Angela Merkel (who, it was learned, hated to be hugged by well-wishers), and Israeli Prime Minister Benjamin Netanyahu, can certainly appreciate the risk of their closest ally revealing their secrets, too.

But there are other facts that we have to come to grips with.

Hillary Clinton sent and received information that there is no way we would ever want our enemies to see. It extends from what we know about terrorist movements around the world to destabilizing issues that threaten our allies to the names of individuals who are risking their lives to help this country by providing us intelligence that can help our friends or thwart our enemies.

If those communications were to fall into the wrong hands, the lives of the people secretly assisting the United States would be all but over. It has happened before.

It should be said that this is of course something that Secretary Clinton would never want to occur. But it is what she may have caused to happen. How ironic that her desire for confidentiality almost surely exposed sensitive information in places where we would never want it to go or revealed the identities and cost the lives of brave men and women who trusted the United States to keep them safe from people who would hunt them down and kill them.

If only Hillary Clinton had been as determined to safeguard the United States' secrets with as much care as she sought to conceal her own.

Reform, Repair, and Open Government

While we are dealing with the public, political, and security fallout of Hillary Clinton's acts, US leaders should already have committed themselves to reform what went wrong, bring about a measure of repair, and reassert the people's right to open government.

That is because what Hillary did wasn't just careless, selfish, or even illegal; it was a violation of the core concept of public service.

She placed her own interest ahead of America's.

Her inherent conflict of interest was also worse than common corner-cutting. By putting her secrets and those of the United States into direct conflict—Clinton committed an unthinkably irresponsible act for anyone in government.

This is because with great power comes perhaps even greater responsibility—and greater shame when the spirit of both is violated.

The fact is, laws are there for a reason. First, they provide a sound structure so our government can operate in a way that meets an appropriate standard of transparency and confidentiality. But they also do something else: they bind us together in a way to keep faith with public accountability, record keeping, and the high honor of government service.

When any of us is given the privilege of serving this country in any of a thousand different ways, we share an obligation to the country's well-being. That is why what is expected of a senior member of Congress and of an entry-level clerk just beginning her civil service career have a great deal in common. Separated by so much, that congressman and clerk are both duty bound to place—at all times—the national interest above their own.

This is a standard that Hillary Clinton not only violated in total but didn't even try to meet. She never had any intention of playing by the rules that govern 100,000 other federal officials who work to meet them every day.

She stood by while underlings and even colleagues lost their careers and their good names for acts a fraction as serious as her own. And when what she had done finally slipped out into the open, her reply to all was a gamut of excuses, distractions, and outright lies. The American people have certainly taken notice.

Every survey taken shows that Hillary Clinton is viewed by the public as dishonest and untrustworthy. As a jury, the public's verdict has very much been rendered.

CHAPTER TWELVE

Bank Accounts as Political Weapons

U nder "Operation Choke Point," beginning in early 2013, the Department of Justice began targeting what it deemed "high-risk" businesses. It didn't directly confront them for wrongdoing themselves, but took the passive-aggressive route of "warning" their banks that they might have accounts belonging to suspicious or illicit businesses. DOJ and federal banking regulators began by sending letters to banks warning that certain of their depositors were in "high-risk" industries. At the urging of the Obama administration, the Federal Deposit Insurance Corporation and the Federal Reserve Board of Governors, cooperating with DOJ, sent financial institutions at least fifty-five administrative subpoenas, demanding confidential documents and information about their clients, without those clients being formally accused of any crime. Many banks, understandably, began responding by sending those businesses letters informing them that their accounts were being terminated, in some cases after decades of doing business with them.

As with the IRS crackdown on Tea Party groups, it appears that pressure to pursue those "high-risk" businesses came from above—including, at least in spirit, from the president. Just as the Citizens United decision was viewed as a crisis by the left, one that demanded some sort of "fix," the financial crisis of 2008 demanded a response. Within a year of his election, President Obama created the Financial Fraud Enforcement Task Force.

For regulators and law enforcement, Wall Street is not as easy a target as small businesses such as payday lenders. And to many people, payday lenders bear at least a symbolic resemblance to the credit card companies and banks involved in the larger crisis of debt and bad mortgages. For a populace newly and rightly suspicious of high-interest loans and easy credit, payday lenders would be a convenient villain. They would also be easy targets for Operation Choke Point.

The Financial Fraud Enforcement Task Force executive director, Michael Bresnick, told a Washington, DC, audience in March 2013 that the task force "focused on financial institutions and payment processors . . . because they are the so-called bottlenecks, or choke-points, in the fraud committed by so many merchants that victimize consumers and launder their illegal proceeds."[1]

DOJ's warnings to banks—combined with banks closing accounts—maintain the appearance of a hands-off approach: no arrests, no prosecutions. But behind that facade is a very troubling disregard for legal due process. The government has immense power to stigmatize and intimidate. Imagine if the government, without passing a specific law against any of your activities or issuing a fine, were to make periodic announcements by loudspeaker in your neighborhood telling everyone that they might want to think twice before doing business with you, since future criminal charges could be coming and you are a risky investment.

Avoiding this sort of arbitrary, ambiguous use of government power is exactly why we have *due process*—clear laws, predictable procedures, predictable punishments, at least in theory. It's much harder to get one's day in court if there is no court, only a sudden letter from one's bank inspired by a vague paranoia. Yet the primitive (and understandable) desire to do the right thing often overwhelms and sweeps aside more abstract, complicated, slow-moving things such as laws. And what looks like an appealing solution in the short run can further empower a runaway executive branch in the long run.

The law that contributed to the long-run problem in this case was in fact older than the 2008 financial crisis, though that crisis gave the government a new reason to flex its muscles. Congress enacted the Financial Institutions Reform, Recovery and Enforcement Act (FIRREA) in 1989 in response to the savings and loan crisis of the 1980s. Section 951 of the law was intended to give DOJ the power to act against individuals and groups that committt fraud *against banks themselves* or that commit mail and wire fraud "affecting a federally insured financial institution."

The DOJ admitted internally that Section 951 did not appear intended to punish organizations committing fraud against their own customers, let alone organizations merely operating in industries where *some* businesses engage in fraud. As one memo conceded, "FIRREA penalties are paid to the Treasury, and the statute does not include a provision for restitution of victims of fraud." Yet now some out-of-favor organizations might be pressured out of business, and in the rare cases in which prosecutions followed, the federal treasury would reap the rewards.

DOJ never attempted to explain why payday lending and payment processing, which are both legal practices even if they aren't considered classy by the elite, were targeted for "choking off." Short-term lending was a particular focus. DOJ seemed more interested in sending a message—directly to banks and only indirectly to payday lenders—than in building real legal cases. DOJ emails from 2013 further suggest that it offered banks a tempting alternative to the risk of further investigations: implement broad policies at the bank by dropping whole categories of businesses. And so the banks did. Yet this is not consistent with DOJ's insistence that it was trying to avoid targeting legal businesses.

With this sort of broad-brush approach, the government could pressure all sorts of corporations, not just banks, into adopting policies that the government prefers, in return for being left alone thereafter. This is a disturbing precedent. Banks could simply be told, say, that sex-related or gun-related businesses seem fishy to the government (since there is a small but real historical risk of such businesses having Mafia ties) and that the banks ought perhaps to err on the safe side by not letting such businesses open accounts with them. The government would be able to maintain a thin pretense of not even putting any real legal pressure on such businesses—neither arrests nor even regulations or fines—while crippling those businesses' ability to function by impeding their relationships with banks. Unless those businesses just want to stuff cash into their mattresses, that is—but that hardly seems like a way to make their accounting practices *more* legitimate.

DOJ recognized the danger of impairing legitimate businesses, saying in a late 2013 memorandum, "Although we recognize the possibility that banks may have therefore decided to stop doing business with legitimate lenders, we do not believe that such decisions should alter our investigative plans. Solving that problem—if it exists—should be left to the legitimate lenders themselves."[2] DOJ's suggestion: let legitimate businesses come up with ways to prove to banks that they are above-board. A simple rule indeed: guilty until proven innocent, without even going before a judge.

The IRS, not surprisingly, has recently engaged in similar tactics. It has been seizing bank accounts of businesses that routinely make deposits smaller than $10,000, on the grounds that narrowly avoiding the threshold at which reporting requirements kick in is itself a suspicious activity.

Among the IRS targets were Maryland dairy farmers Randy and Karen Sowers. As recounted in a letter from House Ways and Means Oversight Subcommittee Chairman Peter Roskam to Treasury Secretary Jacob Lew seeking relief for the couple, Randy Sowers testified before the committee that:

> The IRS seized $67,000 from his farm's account in 2012 because his wife, Karen, often made large cash deposits of proceeds from farmer's markets. A bank teller told Mrs. Sowers that it would reduce paperwork if she deposited the funds in increments under $10,000. Mrs. Sowers did so, believing she was making life easier for the teller, not because she intended to violate federal law. Then, in the course of settlement negotiations, Mr. Sowers told their story to a reporter who published an article on the Sowers' plight. The attorney prosecuting the case then stated in an e-mail that the terms of the settlement agreement were harsher than in other, similar cases because Mr. Sowers had exercised his First Amendment right and spoken to the press. Ultimately, the Sowers settled their case for $29,500 because they needed the remainder of the funds to run their farm.[3]

At least the IRS was pressured into apologizing for the practice, with Commissioner Koskinen telling members of Roskam's committee on the same day Randy Sowers testified in February 2015, "To anyone who is not treated fairly under the code, I apologize." And well he should. Under this account-seizure practice, IRS needs to give neither warning before seizing an account nor proof of wrongdoing.

Even after apologizing, though, Koskinen implied that due process isn't really necessary since, "In 60% of those cases, the owner of the asset never shows up, which shows that they obviously had a criminal activity going on."[4] That's a frightening attitude, and it does not inspire confidence in the IRS's other activities during Koskinen's time as commissioner.

And of course, if the $10,000 reporting threshold had been properly indexed for inflation, the Sowerses would not have been caught in the costly bureaucratic trap in the first place. The $10,000 reporting threshold was set in 1970 with the adoption of the Bank Secrecy Act and has never been raised. As a consequence, millions of honest Americans—like the Sowerses—are now exposed to a law that was originally enacted to allow law enforcement to track and disrupt the finances of a few large criminal enterprises.

The Federal Deposit Insurance Corporation, meant to protect banking customers, not arbitrarily harass them, was a partner with DOJ in Operation Choke Point and in March 2015 ended up being grilled about it by the House Financial Services Subcommittee on Oversight and Investigations. Cochair Sean Duffy (R-WI) told FDIC chairman Martin Gruenberg, "This is not the old Soviet Union or Venezuela or Cuba. I think it's important for all Americans to stand up and push back on policies that are an abuse of government."[5] An array of witnesses testified about the devastating impact of Choke

Point on their businesses. They were hardly shadowy criminals flee-
ing into the night at the first sign of standard accounting practices.

Documents provided to us on the Oversight Committee show
that it was the FDIC that created the list of "high-risk" industries
that was then used to generate DOJ subpoenas. There were numerous meetings between FDIC and DOJ officials in the spring of 2013
to work out details and broad theories. When DOJ sent subpoenas
to banks warning them of potential investigations into "high-risk"
businesses, they attached the FDIC's list of such businesses, as I was
informed by a whistle-blower. One FDIC counsel likened the cozy
relationship with DOJ on this project to "our DOJ/Spike Lee joint."

An official guidance document from FDIC in 2011 notes, "Businesses with elevated risk may include offshore companies, online
gambling-related operations, and on-line payday lenders. Other
businesses with elevated risks include credit repair schemes, debt
consolidation and forgiveness, pharmaceutical sales, telemarket-
ing entities, and online sale of tobacco products."[6] One FDIC official even suggested putting that list on the cover of FDIC's periodic
bulletin to financial institutions, just to make sure the message got
across.

In some cases, the inclusion of companies in the "high-risk"
category did not even seem to be based on their financial dealings.
So, for instance, at the same time as the administration's broader
antigun push was taking place, gun-related businesses were lumped
into the "high-risk" category, again with predictable ripple effects
on private organizations' behavior that was not *directly* decreed by
law or regulation. Training packages for banks' regulatory compliance officers were soon warning, as one guide put it, that "Arms and
ammunition dealers are identified as higher risk because they have
a higher risk of being associated with terrorism and terrorist acts."

That's true, in a very broad sense—but a sense so broad that it is a bit like arresting every citizen of a certain town that is known to have a high overall crime rate. That is not justice.

American Bankers Association president Frank Keating called Operation Choke Point "legally dubious," but the law professor and columnist Glenn Reynolds may have best captured its troubling long-term implications (and underscored a bipartisan danger) when he wrote in *USA Today* that "while abortion clinics and environmental groups are probably safe under the Obama administration, if this sort of thing stands, they will be vulnerable to the same tactics if a different administration adopts this same thuggish approach toward the businesses that it dislikes."[7]

In the case of the IRS, there are periodic calls to restrain its power, even an occasional call for its abolition. In the case of DOJ and FDIC's Choke Point program, a bipartisan coalition of legislators cosponsored a bill to rein in abuses. The Oversight Committee's report helped spur both the House Judiciary Committee and the House Financial Services Committee to hold hearings of their own on Choke Point. Republicans on the Senate Banking Committee condemned Choke Point in a late-2014 letter to the attorney general. And more than thirty members of Congress urged the inspectors general of DOJ and the FDIC to make their own investigations into the program.

DOJ released a statement saying that it had not issued new subpoenas under the program since 2013, and the FDIC officially withdrew its "high-risk" merchants list. Meanwhile, a lawsuit against federal regulators was brought by the Community Financial Services Association of America, with amicus briefs filed by varied groups including the state of South Carolina, the Third Party

Payment Processors Association, the National Organization of African-Americans in Housing, a former chairman of the FDIC, and a Hispanic business group. The problem did not simply go away, and there were sporadic reports of unexplained account closings. Today, however, many people recognize the program's great potential for abuse.

It's an excellent start.

CHAPTER THIRTEEN

Bank Bailouts: Exposed but Unstoppable

A s I write this, I'm serving my eighth term and fifteenth year in the House of Representatives. But even if I serve another fifteen years—or fifty—I do not believe I will ever see a greater rush to judgment and a more severe stampeding of common sense than Washington's panicked reaction to the financial crisis of 2008 and its omnibus spending "solution" known as the Troubled Asset Relief Program, or TARP.

It was one of those perfect political storms where on one side were a Republican White House, Democrat majorities in both houses of Congress, GOP minority leaders on the Hill, the Federal Reserve Bank, what was left of Wall Street, and both party's candidates for president all in favor of the biggest bailout in history.

On the other side? A few Republican and Democrat members with clear doubts that grew into deep misgivings and finally coalesced into bipartisan opposition against all that power—and almost brought it down.

I don't think Washington has been quite the same since.

Though what came to be known as the Financial Crisis of 2008 was indeed a national and even international event, my first awareness of it probably occurred in 2007 in my hometown of Cleveland, Ohio. The occasion was a field hearing of the Oversight Committee that took place there, and the person who took us there was one of the most liberal (and most sincere) members of the House of Representatives, Dennis Kucinich (D-OH). He was elected mayor of Cleveland at the age of thirty-one and, after a very colorful career in and out of politics, was now a member of Congress.

I was excited to attend the hearing and of course to see the old city—but it was anything but an enjoyable trip. The hearing revealed that there was a housing bubble bursting all over the city—and though Kucinich harshly blamed the role of the banks, I was also troubled by what I was hearing: local lenders, as well as community leaders and social service entities, were describing a wave of people turning back their homes to the banks that held their loans because they couldn't afford the mortgages.

Some mortgages were for as little as $300 a month on a $30,000 mortgage.

How could so many people lose so many homes for failing to pay mortgages that were affordable to almost anyone with a job? The answer, we were told, is that very often they were second homes or investment properties and the owners had planned on "flipping" them—buying the home and quickly selling it for a tidy profit based upon an unshakable faith in the ever-increasing value of real estate.

Dennis regarded the plight of those people as a progressive would—as the fault of greedy lenders and heartless banks. I heard the same stories but from the perspective of a businessman. One adage quickly came to mind: Greed drives people to make investments; fear drives them out.

What I was seeing in Cleveland was the aftereffect of greed on the part of realtors, bankers, and individuals, as well as the government backers of those wild loans: Fannie Mae and Freddie Mac. Now fear was causing people to flee their investments.

But the community was the true victim. And soon enough, we would see many more victims in many more communities.

If anyone could get a mortgage on any home—while demonstrating little or no income or assets—what would happen when the Ponzi scheme ceased to work? Though it was true that some of the people who were walking away from the homes were individuals in difficult circumstances or down on their luck, some were realtors, investors, speculators, even real estate novices. And they were only the tip of the iceberg.

Before the hearing, I had rented a car, and as I drove down the most prominent streets in Cleveland—Carnegie, Superior, Sinclair—I could see grand boulevards with large homes in what were now blue-collar neighborhoods. Every third or fourth house seemed to have fresh plywood on it—not after a repair but from repossession of the property. You could practically smell the aroma of recently cut pine nailed onto foreclosed house after foreclosed house.

From that moment, and through the hearing, I knew we had a problem. Dennis Kucinich may have been a progressive liberal with an economic philosophy I did not share, but he was definitely onto something. Because he wasn't a budget guru or close to his party's leadership, he was, perhaps, an imperfect messenger. But that day, he was like the canary in the coal mine. He was a visionary. And he was right.

Unfortunately, not enough people (and very few in Washington) were noticing or listening.

With the series of events leading up to TARP very well documented, the only observation I wish to add is that my colleagues stood by with no emergency hearing but with an emergency interest in what they had heard from the realtors and home builders who were constituents of their individual districts. This type of informed yet anecdotal communication is all too typical of Congress. It is typical of the people whom members of Congress from both parties most often see and most frequently listen to. This is a bipartisan reality.

Similarly, the banks, the Fed, and the mortgage companies had all had plenty of notice that the housing bubble was bursting—not only in Cleveland but all around the world. The problem was real.

In the fall of 2008, as the collapse of the venerable Wall Street investment firm Bear Stearns was happening quickly and completely, indicating that perhaps much worse would be coming soon, emergency meetings on the Hill began. Even though there was a presidential campaign entering its final home stretch, few people yet thought that the housing crisis would be a big factor in it. If individual members felt that the looming economic troubles would affect their reelection, I didn't notice it.

In fact, I don't think Congress focused on the problem in its entirety until the request for money began to develop and finally arrive from the administration in the form of an appropriation to buy "troubled assets"—essentially failed investments, uncollectable loans, and other big, bad bets—from some of the largest and most prominent players in the financial world. The response to it all by the Bush administration was a full spectrum of jargon meant to inspire Congress to do whatever it asked. And it worked.

We were told that "the markets were locking up" and there was "going to be a need for capital." The call for money in large amounts with no strings attached and for the vague reason of locked-up markets was all that many of us had to hear to know we were about to make a large mistake. Every request for a blank check—no matter the amount—is cause for alarm. But a blank check for $700 billion? That's worthy of an alarm louder than any Directed Electronics product we ever installed on a car.

The usual posture of Congress when asked to approve a large spending amount is to compile a long list of "line items"; that is, a series of specifics, lots of detail, and a description of how to move money around with some degree of accountability. This was not that. Before we ever saw even a quickly cobbled-together bill, we were told that the money was not to bail out the banks but for the very vague purpose of "stabilizing the market." That set off more alarms.

If the Bush administration had justified TARP as a necessary measure to bail out the banks, Democrats would have united in opposition. If they had not invented a market economy rationale for the expenditure of billions of dollars, Republicans would have taken a walk because it violated our taboo against throwing money at a problem. And so the mantra "stabilize the markets" was born. If the administration had spray-painted the words on the walls of Congress, it wouldn't have been any more obvious that a first-rate sales job was well under way.

The only problem at that point was that the administration didn't seem to know what it was going to do with the money, either. If the money would truly give confidence to the market, perhaps the idea had merit—as a sort of bridge loan of liquidity. But why $700 billion? Why not $1 trillion? Why not $300 billion? No answer was forthcoming.

Many colleagues in the House noticed this, didn't feel right about it, and decided to join together and see if our suspicions were justified. This included Republicans and Democrats who seemingly didn't share any other views in common—especially on economic matters. But there were two reasons why members enlisted almost from the start.

Those of us on the right were concerned that Congress had never appropriated $700 billion in one lump sum, even in time of war, to be spent as seen fit by a few officials appointed by the president. Even in war, Congress has traditionally asked for and been told the number of tanks, the amount of munitions, and so on when approving the most vital funding requests. That wasn't happening here. The level of accountability would be zero.

A distrust of big banks and Wall Street drove my liberal colleagues' opposition to what they could see was a handout, one made on the promise that it would be well spent to purchase troubled assets and credit instruments selling at a "market amount." We asked what the "market amount" was, and the administration experts said they couldn't say because at the moment we were in a "dysfunctional market."

They could never define what they would be paying for the troubled assets and which ones they would buy. It was that murky and that mysterious. But one thing was clearer than all others: TARP was essentially being used as a safety net for the bad bets and losing calls of some of the most prominent and powerful financial players in the country and in the world. When they took risks and did well, they pocketed the money. When their reckless wagers or shady maneuvers blew up or went bad, American taxpayers were expected to pay for the losses.

No croupier in Las Vegas is going to keep covering your losing roulette wagers until the wheel stops on 22 black so you can walk away a winner. In that way, TARP violated every principle of economic investment and destroyed the kind of discipline we should be encouraging. If there aren't consequences as well as rewards in the investment world, we will simply cease to have a reliable free market.

We began to feel as though the taxpayers were the ones paying for someone else's bad bets. Legislation was hastily crafted, not in Congress but in the White House. That's important, because it lacked any semblance of useful accountability. As a practical matter, the spending of the entire $700 billion was left entirely up to the president—a Republican president, in this case. That is why the fight against TARP was, ultimately, a fight against my own party.

My view is that President Bush relied far too much upon very knowledgeable but somewhat conflicted financial advisers: the chairman of the Federal Reserve System, Ben Bernanke, and Secretary of the Treasury Henry Paulson, a former CEO of the Wall Street giant Goldman Sachs. The chairman of the New York Federal Reserve was also an extremely enthusiastic backer. His name was Tim Geithner. By no small coincidence, he would next hold the title of Treasury secretary.

We were told to approve the appropriation, do it quickly, and then shut up about it. It didn't feel right. Again and again, Paulson told us that the country was facing a "crisis of confidence." I certainly agreed with him, although not in the way he intended. The real crisis was that TARP failed every test of appropriateness. But what to do about it?

Just days before we were to vote to approve the measure, an opinion essay that changed everything appeared in the *Washington Post*. The author was Bill Isaac, the former chairman of the Federal Deposit Insurance Corporation. And he was saying we didn't have to do it.

He started getting phone calls from various members of Congress—Democrats Marcy Kaptur of Ohio, Brad Sherman of California, and John Hall of New York, as well as from his own congressman, my Republican colleague Vern Buchanan of Florida. Though we were all skeptical of Paulson's plan, Isaac remembers, my colleagues seemed especially frustrated that leaders from both our parties were determined to force a quick yes vote on TARP before any reasonable hearing process, with no real debate and zero accountability. I also reached out to him courtesy of my old friend Peter Tanous, a financial expert and one of the authors of the excellent book *The End of Prosperity: How Higher Taxes Will Doom the Economy—If We Let It Happen*. We all urged Isaac to come to Washington and join the fight against TARP, but he put us off.

"Congress is going to approve the bailout bill on Monday," he said, "and my presence in Washington is not going to change anything. We are taking the kids to see the Buccaneers play the Packers tomorrow, and that's a much better way for me to spend my weekend." Finally he gave in. Sometimes members of Congress can be persistent.

Of note is the fact that this was all happening on a Saturday—not usually a busy workday for the Congress. The next day was Sunday, September 28, and Isaac flew to Washington. My office became the center of the fight against TARP, and my staff put the word out that Isaac was ready to meet with any member of Congress, Democrat or Republican, to discuss any aspect of the financial crisis and any detail of the proposed bailout.

All that day, Isaac met with members of Congress from every part of the political spectrum. I even visited the House Progressive Caucus, the first and last time I was welcomed in that room as an ally.

In the end, he met with more than two hundred members, including an unforgettable briefing with Jesse Jackson of Illinois and Maxine Waters of California sitting together with several conservative Republicans—all united in their efforts to defeat TARP. The meeting went on until past 1 a.m.

The next day was the vote on TARP, and the leaders of both parties "viewed the skeptics as an annoyance," as Isaac put it, which was an understatement. Word was out that Speaker Nancy Pelosi and others were threatening to revoke members' committee assignments and rescind financial assistance for their reelection.

My California colleague and fellow Republican David Dreier urged me to support TARP because "Hank Paulson told me that if we don't do this, people are going to go to their ATM machines and no money is going to come out." I think that is what they mean by "playing hardball," but I told him it sounded implausible and I simply didn't believe it would happen.

But the vote seemed to be delayed again and again—and the bill was ultimately defeated 228–205. It was an extraordinary defeat for the powers that be but hardly an uplifting victory for our side. There was no joy in stopping that freight train of momentum for a massive mistake. And we suspected we were stopping it for only a while.

In very short order, the losing side demanded a rematch and got it. The pressure to change our opposing votes was enormous. Still, it was not going well for Team TARP.

Even though the GOP was the minority of the House, one of our own sat in the White House, so we were baldly asked to support our Republican friend. And George W. Bush called in favor after favor. For me, one meeting stands out among all the others. It was an invitation to every Republican member of the House, and it was convened in the Cannon Caucus Room—the largest and one of the most ornate meeting rooms used by Congress. How appropriate for the most expensive vote in US history.

It was also a less personal but more comfortable setting for the Bush administration members who were on hand to give us the hard sell—Fed Chairman Ben Bernanke and Treasury Secretary Henry Paulson. Only this time, Vice President Dick Cheney, himself a former member of Congress and at one time the Republican whip of the House of Representatives, was in attendance. He carried a lot of credibility.

They weren't there to allow us to convince them that they were mistaken. Instead, they had made the trip to stake a claim to party loyalty, personal admiration of President Bush, even blind faith in their financial expertise—whatever it took. Cheney looked deeply uncomfortable, his body language giving off clear misgivings about what we were being asked to do. But it was enough. After some additional arm-twisting—as if to the point of bones breaking—some Republicans and Democrats were convinced to change their votes and support TARP. The fight was over.

Was it worth it?

As a practical matter, the spending of the entire $700 billion was left entirely up to the president—and I was opposed to giving that authority to Bush. The reasons became clearer to my GOP colleagues the next year when President Obama used the funds to prepackage Chrysler for sale to Fiat and money that had ostensibly been intended to assist banks was used by General Motors to cover union pensions, but not the nonunion pensions of similar retirees.

In the case of Delphi, a parts distributor for GM, men and women in its plant in Dayton, Ohio, who had worked side by side were treated completely differently. Obama used just enough bailout funds to cover pensions for retired Delphi workers, but only the union ones. The nonunion retirees? Obama didn't take care of them. They were out of the money promised for their retirement, after it was too late to go back to work. TARP made it possible.

TARP was wrong in principle and wrong in practice. It was bad politics and even worse policy. For those who got some of its billions—including the well connected on Wall Street and the well thought of among Democrats—the bailout was a blowout. But for those who were shut out of its largesse or who weren't "important enough" to save, TARP was far more and far worse.

Opposing it was absolutely right—and well worth the fight.

CHAPTER FOURTEEN

Turning a Deaf Ear to Whistle-blowers and a Blind Eye to Cover-ups

The attitude of politicians, the media, and the popular culture toward whistle-blowers sure can change dramatically.

Sometimes whistle-blowers are hailed as heroes. By absconding with a trove of Defense Department documents detailing the Vietnam War that became known as the Pentagon Papers and giving them to the *New York Times*, Daniel Ellsberg became one of the most famous (and praised) of all whistle-blowers. Likewise, the then-anonymous Watergate figure known as Deep Throat will be forever portrayed as the great revealer of wrongdoing and enabler of journalistic valor who forced the resignation of a scandal-scathed president.

More recently, in 2002, three women, including an FBI agent who wrote a blistering memo on intelligence failures at the bureau and two others who exposed corporate corruption at Enron and WorldCom were even named *Time* magazine's "Persons of the

Year." The cover photo accompanying the story—entitled "The Whistle-Blowers"—features all three, arms crossed, looking serious, determined, and impressive.

By contrast, Democrat Senator Harry Reid condemned as "a bunch of whiners" more than a dozen whistle-blowers at the Department of Homeland Security who accused him of pressuring the department to expedite the visa paperwork for well connected applicants. Where was the DHS employees' defense in the media? Where was *their* perfectly lit newsmagazine cover?

Sometimes the mainstream media treats as virtues the full disclosure of public documents and compliance with legally issued congressional subpoenas. When Nixon resisted turning over the tapes that ultimately forced his resignation, the entire media establishment proclaimed—in unison—that the people had a right to know what he knew and when he'd known it.

The investigation into Benghazi was repeatedly frustrated by Hillary Clinton's State Department—with sporadic and odd revelations, such as former Clinton adviser Sidney Blumenthal giving her consultations about global espionage and Libyan business opportunities during her time as secretary of state. One ironic result is that all the delaying tactics have managed to drag the Benghazi investigation on longer than the time between the Watergate break-in and Nixon's resignation (another irony is that Clinton got her start as a young lawyer helping to prosecute Nixon).

In recent decades, the courts have arguably tended to be happier when pressing Republican administrations to comply with investigations. Nixon, for good or ill, faced dogged reporters, public outcry, and a full congressional investigation that seemed bent on cornering him. No Democrat has been made to confront all three at once.

In 2006, both the House and Senate Judiciary Committees investigated the Bush administration's firing of US attorneys it had appointed—and the hearings began the month after the dismissals. Resignations of several administration officials involved occurred by late 2007, along with a vote by Congress to hold former White House counsel Harriet Miers in contempt for failing to appear before them and explain whether the firings were her idea. By Washington standards, it was light speed.

If anything, one would think that since Obama promised his would be "the most transparent administration in history," we might see a greater commitment to assist investigations than under Bush—and see even more sympathy for whistle-blowers. But the opposite has been true. The Obama administration has instead persecuted whistle-blowers, stalled their careers, prevented their professional advancement, and tried to badger them into silence—all of it in plain sight.

The truth is that the central importance of whistle-blower protections has a long and honorable place in US history.

Indeed, even during wartime, the first Republican president, Abraham Lincoln, saw the need to protect whistle-blowers and open the books on fraudulent military contractors. He encouraged the passage of the False Claims Act with its *qui tam* provision, meaning that private citizens may file suit in such matters in order to aid prosecutors. Allowing private citizens to acquire information about fraudulent and wasteful government contractors created a precursor of sorts to the Freedom of Information Act (FOIA) requests private citizens can make of government today.

If Congress has any courage at all, it must demonstrate that it is, so to speak, a credible threat to executive-branch agents guilty of malfeasance. The legislative branch is often described as closest to the people, but it can play that role only if it is not supine before an imperial presidency. Strengthening whistle-blower protections while more severely punishing those who obstruct investigations would be a one-two punch of legal reforms putting future executive-branch agents—yes, even Republican ones—on notice that a political appointment does not carry carte blanche to do whatever the president, a cabinet secretary, or another government official desires.

Political winds change direction frequently, but the law endures, and the cause of keeping even the most powerful government appointees from harming their underlings must continue.

Who knows how many times intimidation tactics have succeeded? What our investigations were able to find out, however, is that there are some brave people who are too committed to be easily threatened, too brave to be intimidated. They are the true heroes of much of our truth-seeking work.

When Jeffrey Sterling, a CIA staffer turned leaker, went on trial in early 2015, the CIA seized the opportunity to bring in a parade of witnesses attesting to the good character of the CIA and the wisdom of the plan that had been exposed—giving fake nuclear weapons designs to Iran—while making Sterling sound like a reckless man who had shared vital intelligence with author and *New York Times* reporter James Risen. Yet Sterling was plainly not just blabbing to the world. He initially went through appropriate channels, alerting the Senate Intelligence Committee to what the *New York Times* described as "a CIA operation in which a former Russian scientist provided Iran with intentionally flawed nuclear component schematics"—fake nuclear intelligence secrets. Sterling tried to advance important truths in appropriate ways.

Some analysts now think that the CIA's scheme accelerated the Iranian nuclear program instead of hamstringing it—yet Sterling was convicted not just of leaking but also of espionage, making him only the fifth American charged with espionage in the past century. That's one way our government delivers a message of deterrence to others who might be as inclined as Sterling to aid the cause of public disclosure. Risen has also been pressured by prosecutors to reveal his sources, but the *Times* seems not to have rethought its editorial support for Obama despite his pressuring one of its reporters.

Reasonable people can disagree about whether leaking sensitive national security cases serves the public interest, but it is not just cases like these that have led to punitive or preemptive measures being taken against whistle-blowers. Despite the Obama administration's vow of transparency, executive-branch agencies have become ever more aggressive against leakers, sometimes against whistle-blowers who have been important in Oversight Committee investigations. Managers in several agencies who discovered that their underlings were whistle-blowers appear to have stripped them of responsibilities and thwarted their opportunities for career advancement while carefully avoiding any more overt punishment that could have triggered a lawsuit.

The Oversight Committee learned that the Food and Drug Administration, for instance, goes to great lengths to identify and monitor employees who attempt to communicate directly with Congress—a pattern of managerial misbehavior that threatens to usher in a reign of surveillance tyranny.

That is why, despite nominal protections for whistle-blowers in the case of government malfeasance, it's still far safer to stay on the government's good side than to end up in its crosshairs. Though the government might punish you for spilling its secrets, it is rarely moved to punish government appointees severely for *keeping* secrets—even when the secret kept refers to a crime.

When Lois Lerner's undisclosed emails were found by the Treasury Inspector General for Tax Administration in April 2015, the IRS's official reaction was one for the ages: "We welcome the Inspector General's recovery of these Lois Lerner emails. This is an encouraging development that will help resolve remaining questions and dispel uncertainty surrounding the e-mails." *We welcome?*

Every one of those emails was, by law, supposed to be turned over by the IRS. Every one of them wasn't. Not until the agency's independent watchdog uncovered them did their embarrassing content come to light. Yet I don't recall the inspector general receiving glowing profiles in the *New York Times* or reading any editorial from the Gray Lady insisting that whoever had tried to bury the emails must swiftly be brought to justice.

Worst of all are the ugly, unjust ways in which whistle-blowers who came forward with information about wrongdoing valuable to the Oversight Committee—and the public—have been aggressively punished within Obama's administration. The damage to democracy and transparency is compounded when the initial wrongdoing in question is itself an attempt by a government agency to squelch information disclosure to the public.

The committee also investigated serious political interference with FOIA requests at the Department of Homeland Security.

One witness in the case, Catherine Popoi, was interviewed by the committee on March 3, 2011, and *the very next day* was contacted by the DHS's deputy chief privacy officer and told that she would be demoted ten days later, made subordinate to a recently created layer of the DHS hierarchy, and moved into an office that had once belonged to someone who worked under her.

We learned that those changes had been decided upon a full two months earlier in case Popoi continued talking to the Oversight

Committee. When she told the truth, she was told she was being demoted. Is it any wonder that some potential whistle-blowers choose silence over a damaged career?

At Hillary Clinton's State Department during the investigation of the Benghazi attacks, so many potential witnesses told the committee about their fear of reprisals from superiors that I requested that the State Department's principal deputy legal adviser make clear to all employees that they are entitled by law to furnish information to Congress that they think is necessary to serve public safety and the national interest. State never even took that small step—and as a result has abetted the intimidation of potential whistle-blowers and the denial of information the public has a right to know.

Victoria Toensing, the attorney for one Benghazi witness, said State Department officials have made "some very despicable threats" to potential witnesses, "taking career people and making them well aware their careers will be over" if they cooperate with the Oversight Committee.[1]

Former Deputy Chief of Mission in Libya Gregory Hicks, the last person to speak to slain Ambassador Chris Stevens during the attacks that claimed his life, was demoted after talking to the committee. The leftist magazine *The Nation* admirably argued that even if one is not a supporter of the Republican Congress and disagrees with Hicks's assessment of the Benghazi debacle, everyone should be troubled by the retaliation he appears to have faced for talking about it.

Similarly, ATF agent John Dodson, a crucial Fast and Furious witness for the committee, appears to have faced coordinated retaliation from the government itself and from its allies in the media. We learned that the Justice Department released internal documents about Dodson to the press in an effort to undermine his credibility.

And it worked. Katherine Eban, a former Bill Clinton campaign worker turned writer for the *New York Times*, *Fortune*, and other outlets, for instance, wrote an article portraying Dodson in a negative light, which I believe was a clear misrepresentation of the facts.

To the Obama administration—and by extension the media— leaking about possible government wrongdoing is frowned upon, but leaking about the leakers is a cause that rallies administration allies. Such is life as a whistle-blower during the Obama administration, and it's important to note that there are whistle-blowers who remain in their jobs today but are isolated, shunned, and blocked from career advancement. I'm exceptionally proud that my current staffers (as well as former associates who have gone on to other positions in Congress) are ever vigilant in attempting to shield whistle-blowers—with varied success.

What is needed now are updated ways to consistently and constantly monitor and protect whistle-blowers both in and out of government and a promise from every congressional chairman and leader to have a dedicated passion to protect whistle-blowers.

We need this because Gregory Hicks, John Dodson, Catherine Popoi, and all the others who stepped forward with the truth and were attacked for it know by now that they will not likely be feted as *Time* magazine's "Persons of the Year." *Vanity Fair* isn't calling to schedule glamorous photo sessions showcasing them dramatically posing in front of Washington's landmarks against a sunset background. ABC, CBS, and NBC have all passed on creating a heroic and thrilling documentary of their life stories and what they did to strike a blow for the people. No glamorous actor or actress is seen tweeting how wonderful they are and publicly asking to portray them in a movie chronicling their courage against the absolute power of an out-of-control government.

Perhaps this will change, but the odds are that they won't be given any of those benefits. But they should have something even more valuable: our gratitude and admiration for doing the right thing, braving harsh consequences, ensuring that accountability exists, and giving truth its turn.

CHAPTER FIFTEEN

Why the Oversight Committee Keeps Watch

An emerging challenge for reformers, which requires an ambitious set of reforms, is the limited power of the Oversight Committee. We could subpoena witnesses and documents. We could urge that those who did not cooperate or who lied to the committee be found in contempt of Congress. Yet we had no real enforcement power to compel government officials to come forward and tell the truth. No one went to jail for refusing to appear before the Oversight Committee. I don't relish the prospect of anyone doing so, but given the seriousness of the wrongdoing being investigated in some of these cases, I do wish executive-branch appointees took the responsibility of testifying more seriously.

Though Hillary Clinton manages to talk as if her use of private email for State Department business was a casual, barely significant decision made by a technologically unsophisticated person for reasons of convenience and efficiency, she cannot plausibly deny that she was aware that the Oversight Committee was attempting to determine whether private email accounts were being used for such purposes.

That is her great lie. The Oversight Committee sent letters to numerous cabinet-level officials on December 13, 2012, seven weeks prior to her departure from the State Department, asking whether any of these officials or their underlings used private email accounts for government business, what those private email addresses were, and whether they were accessible by the Oversight Committee. She received one of those letters.

DARRELL E. ISSA, CALIFORNIA
CHAIRMAN

DAN BURTON, INDIANA
JOHN L. MICA, FLORIDA
TODD RUSSELL PLATTS, PENNSYLVANIA
MICHAEL R. TURNER, OHIO
PATRICK McHENRY, NORTH CAROLINA
JIM JORDAN, OHIO
JASON CHAFFETZ, UTAH
CONNIE MACK, FLORIDA
TIM WALBERG, MICHIGAN
JAMES LANKFORD, OKLAHOMA
JUSTIN AMASH, MICHIGAN
ANN MARIE BUERKLE, NEW YORK
PAUL A. GOSAR, D.D.S., ARIZONA
RAUL R. LABRADOR, IDAHO
PATRICK MEEHAN, PENNSYLVANIA
SCOTT DesJARLAIS, M.D. TENNESSEE
JOE WALSH, ILLINOIS
TREY GOWDY, SOUTH CAROLINA
DENNIS A. ROSS, FLORIDA
FRANK C. GUINTA, NEW HAMPSHIRE
BLAKE FARENTHOLD, TEXAS
MIKE KELLY, PENNSYLVANIA

LAWRENCE J. BRADY
STAFF DIRECTOR

ONE HUNDRED TWELFTH CONGRESS

Congress of the United States
House of Representatives

COMMITTEE ON OVERSIGHT AND GOVERNMENT REFORM
2157 RAYBURN HOUSE OFFICE BUILDING
WASHINGTON, DC 20515–6143

MAJORITY (202) 225-5074
FACSIMILE (202) 225-3974
MINORITY (202) 225-5051

http://oversight.house.gov

ELIJAH E. CUMMINGS, MARYLAND
RANKING MINORITY MEMBER

EDOLPHUS TOWNS, NEW YORK
CAROLYN B. MALONEY, NEW YORK
ELEANOR HOLMES NORTON,
DISTRICT OF COLUMBIA
DENNIS J. KUCINICH, OHIO
JOHN F. TIERNEY, MASSACHUSETTS
WM. LACY CLAY, MISSOURI
STEPHEN F. LYNCH, MASSACHUSETTS
JIM COOPER, TENNESSEE
GERALD E. CONNOLLY, VIRGINIA
MIKE QUIGLEY, ILLINOIS
DANNY K. DAVIS, ILLINOIS
BRUCE L. BRALEY, IOWA
PETER WELCH, VERMONT
JOHN A. YARMUTH, KENTUCKY
CHRISTOPHER S. MURPHY, CONNECTICUT
JACKIE SPEIER, CALIFORNIA

December 13, 2012

The Honorable Jeffrey Zients
Acting Director for Management
Office of Management and Budget
1650 Pennsylvania Ave., NW
Washington, D.C 20503

Dear Mr. Zients:

In conjunction with the Committee's oversight into improprieties associated with the Department of Energy's 1705 Loan Guarantee Program, the issue of the use of personal e-mail accounts to conduct official business arose on numerous occasions.[1] Energy Department employees brazenly used personal e-mail accounts to communicate about internal loan guarantee decisions. In doing so, they circumvented laws and regulations governing recordkeeping requirements, concealed their discussions, and attempted to insulate their communications from scrutiny. For example, Jonathan Silver, a political appointee in charge of the $38 billion program, used his personal account to e-mail another DOE official's personal account, issuing a stern warning: **"Don't ever send an email on doe email with a personal email addresses [sic]. That makes them subpoenable."**[2]

The challenges associated with electronic records preservation, are not limited to the use of personal e-mail. Recently, allegations arose that EPA Administrator Lisa Jackson has used at least one alias e-mail account—under the name "Richard Windsor"—to conduct official business.[3] Such use of an alias raises the potential for inadequate tagging to the proper official and incomplete archiving of these communications.

These examples suggest that the challenges this Administration has faced regarding the preservation of electronic communications used to conduct official business have persisted, rather than improved. Further, the growth of social media platforms—such as Facebook, Twitter, and G-chat—and mobile technologies—including laptops, handheld

---

[1] See, e.g., Letter from Rep. Darrell Issa, Chairman, & Rep. Jim Jordan, Chairman, Subcomm. on Reg. Affairs, Stimulus Oversight, & Gov't Spending, H. Comm. on Oversight & Gov't Reform (OGR), to Richard Kaufmann, Senior Advisor to the Sec'y, U.S. Dep't of Energy, et al (Aug. 15, 2012) (requesting communications from non-official e-mail accounts regarding section 1705 loan guarantee program).

[2] E-mail from Jonathan Silver to Morgan Wright (Aug. 21, 2011).

[3] Brendan Sasso, *House Republicans Question EPA over Secret Email Accounts*, THE HILL, Nov. 17, 2012, http://thehill.com/blogs/e2-wire/e2-wire/268605-republicans-question-epa-over-secrect-email-accounts; Michael Bastasch, *EPA Chiefs Secret 'Alias' E-mail Account Revealed*, DAILY CALLER, Nov. 12, 2012, http://dailycaller.com/2012/11/12/epa-chiefs-secret-alias-email-account-revealed/.

mobile devices, and iPads—pose new challenges for capturing and retaining records under existing federal law.

For some time, the Committee on Oversight and Government reform has been aware of deficiencies in compliance with both the Presidential Records Act and the Federal Records Act. During the 110th Congress, under the leadership of then-Chairman Henry A. Waxman, the Committee sent letters to the heads of 23 Executive Branch departments and agencies regarding e-mail communications using non-official accounts.[4] Early in the Obama Administration, on February 18, 2009, I wrote to Gregory B. Craig, then-Counsel to the President, regarding this very subject.[5] In April 2010, reports emerged that Office of Science and Technology Policy Deputy Chief Technology Officer Andrew McLaughlin had used his personal e-mail account to engage in official business. Specifically, he used his personal account to engage in discussion regarding policy matters under his review with his former employer, Google, Inc.[6] In light of these and other reports documenting transparency failures, I alerted then-Committee Chairman Edolphus Towns of the need to investigate the matter further.[7]

On May 3, 2011, the full Committee held a hearing entitled, "Presidential Records in the New Millennium: Updating the Presidential Records Act and Other Federal Recordkeeping Statutes to Improve Electronic Records Preservation." The hearing examined the enhanced transparency technology offers, particularly to improve citizens' ability to interact with the federal government. It also highlighted the challenge of preventing federal officials from hiding their actions from public scrutiny in spite of these technological advancements. Finally, earlier this year, I wrote to White House Chief of Staff Jack Lew on August 3, 2012, requesting details of the use of personal e-mail accounts by White House staff to conduct official business.[8]

President Obama stressed improving the public's ability to scrutinize government actions and decisions as part of his commitment to having the "most open and transparent [government] in history."[9] The growth of technology, however, continues to create new challenges for electronic records preservation, and this Administration has struggled to ensure that official actions are appropriately captured and documented.

To better assess the extent of this pervasive problem across the Executive Branch, I am writing to request information about your agency's policies and practices regarding the use of personal e-mail and other forms of electronic communication to conduct official

---

[4] See, e.g., Letter from Rep. Henry Waxman, Chairman, OGR, to Hon. Michael Astrue, Comm'r, U.S. Soc. Sec. Admm., et al (Apr. 12, 2007).

[5] Letter from Rep. Darrell Issa, Ranking Mem., OCR, to Hon. Gregory B. Craig, Counsel to the President (Feb. 18, 2009) (requesting detailed information about White House's Presidential Records Act compliance efforts).

[6] Kim Hart, Former Googler To Resign from White House, POLITICO, Dec. 22, 2010, http://www.politico.com/news/stories/1210/46740.html.

[7] See, e.g., Letter from Rep. Darrell Issa, Ranking Mem., OGR, to Rep. Edolphus Towns, Chairman, OGR (June 30, 2010) (requesting investigation of use of personal e-mail accounts by Administration officials reported in media).

[8] Letter from Rep. Darrell Issa, Chairman, OGR, to Hon. Jack Lew, Chief of Staff, The White House (Aug. 3, 2012).

[9] The White House Blog, Change has come to WhiteHousese.gov, http://www.whitehouse.gov/blog/change_has_come_to_whitehouse-gov (Jan. 20, 2009).

Page 3

business. Please provide the following information as soon as possible, but by no later than January 7, 2013:

1. Have you or any senior agency official ever used a personal e-mail account to conduct official business? If so, please identify the account used.

2. Have you or any senior agency official ever used an alias e-mail account to conduct official business? If so, please identify the account used.

3. Have you or any senior agency official ever used text messages, sent from an official or personal device, to conduct official business? If so, please identify the number or account used.

4. Please provide written documentation of the agency's policies regarding the use of non-official e-mail accounts to conduct official business, including, but not limited to, archiving and recordkeeping procedures, as well as disciplinary proceedings for employees in violation of these policies.

5. Does the agency require employees to certify on a periodic basis or at the end of their employment with the agency they have turned over any communications involving official business that they have sent or received using non-official accounts?

6. What is the agency's policy for retention of information posted on social networking platforms, including, but not limited to, Twitter or Facebook?

7. What agency policies and procedures are currently in place to ensure that all messages related to official business sent or received by federal employees and contractors on private, non-governmental e-mail accounts or social networking platforms are properly categorized as federal records?

8. Have any agency employees been subject to disciplinary proceedings for using non-official e-mail accounts to conduct official business since January 20, 2009? If so, please provide a list of names, dates of proceedings, and final outcomes.

The Committee on Oversight and Government Reform is the principal oversight committee of the House of Representatives and may at "any time" investigate "any matter" as set forth in House Rule X.

Please deliver your responses to the Majority Staff in Room 2157 of the Rayburn House Office Building and the Minority Staff in Room 2471 of the Rayburn House Office Building. The Committee prefers to receive all documents in electronic format.

If you have any questions about this request, please call Ashley Callen or John Ohly of the Committee Staff at (202) 225-5074. Thank you for your prompt attention to this matter.

Sincerely,

Darrell Issa
Chairman

cc: The Honorable Elijah E. Cummings, Ranking Minority Member

Secretary Clinton mass-deleted her private emails *after* receiving that request. Her secret system having been exposed, she then also oversaw the separation of those of her emails that were made available to the public and those that she deemed "personal" and then sought to eliminate. This fact may be lost among the big events of an important election, but it is no small matter. The public must realize that they, too, have a stake in not tolerating these and other brazen acts to keep secret what should be known.

It is troubling enough to see government work blend into personal benefits or wheeling and dealing when the result is decadent but in the grand budgetary scheme of things relatively small—such as the Department of Energy's lavish $21 million 2013–2014 budget for Las Vegas parties, golf outings, and casino nights. But when the Oversight Committee and by extension the public cannot be confident that the State Department is conducting itself in an ethical fashion (a fashion not influenced, for instance, by the millions of dollars donated by foreign governments to the Clintons' private foundation), and is knowingly and willfully denied access to the relevant evidence, that is cause for severe alarm.

Clinton is not the only executive-branch official to ignore formal requests from the Oversight Committee, just the most brazen and, because of her reckless handling of national security information, potentially the most dangerous.

Her response at times is to claim to be genuinely puzzled that the country might not believe her credible. The public's reaction is often determined to be—by her supporters and even her detractors—due to "an image problem."

But that is not the case. Hillary Clinton does not have an image problem. She has a truth problem. And a trust problem.

Even as the State Department refused for months to permit

the committee anything more than access to large numbers of poorly organized documents "in camera"—that is, in person, without removing or copying them—officials there sent us messages explaining how fully they believed themselves to be complying, at times little more than boilerplate from their standard email policy, beginning with the assurance on October 12, 2012, that

> We look forward to working with the Congress and your Committee as you proceed with your own review. As you know, we have already begun working with your Committee. We are committed to a process that is as transparent as possible, respecting the needs and integrity of the investigation underway. We will move as quickly as we can without forsaking accuracy.

One thing that Clinton and other officials shouldn't be surprised by is periodic requests for information from the committee. Compliance, if they wanted to comply, would not have been difficult. This matter has dragged on for years because the State Department and the White House wanted it to drag on for years.

The Oversight Committee is not a recent development foisted on the Obama administration by antigovernment zealots. The committee and its precursors have existed in some form since the earliest days of the United States. During the Second Congress, in 1792, President Washington asked the House of Representatives to form a committee to investigate the reasons for a defeat suffered by the army at the Battle of Wabash River during the Northwest Indian War. The original resolution Washington put before Congress suggested avenues of investigation, including looking into delays in delivery of money, military stores, food, and other items.

Even at the risk of causing embarrassment to his own office, Washington wanted answers, and the representatives present officially agreed that "Inquiry into the expenditure of all public money was the indispensable duty of this House." Recognizing the members of the House as "the immediate guardians of the public interest," the resolution granted the committee the power to "call for such persons, papers, and records, as may be necessary to assist their inquiries." By a 44–10 vote, the first oversight committee was created.

The difference between President Washington's leadership in revealing circumstances and the lack thereof by current and potentially future inhabitants of the office should not be ignored.

It was followed by institutions such as the Committee on Expenditures during the War of 1812, meant "to examine into the state of the departments and of appropriation laws, to watch for violations of the law in expenditures, and to report provisions looking to economy and to accountability of public officers."

Over the course of the next 115 years, that original committee divided into multiple committees tasked with overseeing different executive-branch agencies, so that there was one oversight committee each for watching over the expenditures of the Departments of State, Treasury, War, and the Navy, plus oversight committees for the Post Office and Public Buildings, and from the Civil War until World War I one Committee on Expenditures each for Interior, Justice, Agriculture, Commerce and Labor, and later Labor as a separate department. In 1927, those were fused into the Committee on Expenditures and Executive Departments, renamed the Committee on Government Operations in 1952, the Committee on Government Reform and Oversight in 1994, the Committee on Government Reform in 2001, and the Committee on Oversight and Government Reform in 2007.

I served as the committee's top Republican for six years, from 2009 to 2015, all but the first two years, when Democrats held the House, as chairman.

At the times when the White House and Congress are controlled by different parties, each may think of oversight investigations as a nuisance created by the other party, but as Supreme Court Chief Justice Earl Warren put it:

> The power of the Congress to conduct investigations is inherent in the legislative process. That power is broad. It encompasses inquiries concerning the administration of existing laws, as well as proposed or possibly needed statutes. It includes surveys of defects in our social, economic or political system for the purpose of enabling the Congress to remedy them. It comprehends probes into departments of the Federal Government to expose corruption, inefficiency or waste.[1]

The Oversight Committee has legislative jurisdiction over issues related to "government management and accounting measures generally." It has a special mandate to conduct comprehensive oversight on all levels of government, even as other committees oversee specific activities and subject areas.

Furthermore, as the House's chief investigative body, the House rules say that the committee may investigate "any matter" at "any time" for any reason and, in an independent fashion that few other parts of government can, to make "the findings and recommendations of the committee" available "to any other standing committee having jurisdiction over the matter involved." This also means that as much as it might surprise many of the witnesses we summon, Congress has the right to "require, by subpoena or otherwise, the attendance and testimony of such witnesses and the production of such books, records, correspondence, memorandums, papers, documents and other materials as it considers necessary."[2]

Over the four years I was chairman, the committee sent more than two thousand letters requesting information from government agencies, officials, and interested parties and issued more than one hundred subpoenas compelling the production of documents—such as emails about the government's handling of the Benghazi attacks, Fast and Furious, and other contentious events. We rarely started off with a subpoena, choosing first to write a letter explaining the committee's interest and requesting information and documents from agencies or other interests.

Subpoenas were issued only when there wasn't voluntary cooperation or when we faced intentional efforts to thwart the committee's oversight efforts. At other times, we issued "friendly" subpoenas to parties, usually government contractors, who requested them because they feared retaliation from agency officials if they appeared to be cooperating with the committee's efforts. That was the case with some HealthCare.gov contractors.

Tensions within the committee complicated our efforts, though, and, as I mentioned earlier, had been heightened by the Democrats' insistence that the often combative Representative Cummings would be ranking member instead of my predecessor as chairman, the more congenial Representative Towns (though, on the bright side, clashes with Cummings were purely public ones that resulted in no real personal animosity between us behind the scenes). Knowing that they had a staunch defender in Cummings no doubt emboldened administration officials to resist requests from Oversight. When the committee is not united, it is much more difficult to do important parts of its work.

The minority during my tenure was reluctant, for instance, to grant immunity to some whistle-blowers who had essential information the public deserved to know and was prepared to tell.

When the Democrats were in the majority, of course, it was even easier for them to defend the president. During the 2009 investigation of ACORN, for instance, even the committee's chief investigator didn't seem to see what the big deal was—and as a member of the then-minority, I wasn't even allowed to call witnesses. That made it hard to dig up the facts.

But I believe we always treated the committee as something with a mission that easily transcended mere partisanship. We were passionate about it, in fact. And to be honest, even when we were aghast at government officials' bad behavior, we had fun doing what we believe is very important and rewarding work.

The stonewalling of investigations, however, isn't something that affects only the Oversight Committee. Among other things, government's disregard for even the concept of oversight can increase its arrogance in dealing with other sorts of investigators.

Take, for instance, the undermining of inspectors general.

Though I would hardly blame cynical members of the public for wondering if the government can ever truly investigate itself, the inspectors general of each department, much like the Oversight Committee and special prosecutors, have functioned as extremely useful voices, and we should be very grateful for what they do.

In fiscal year 2015, for example, inspectors general helped identify some $51.8 billion in potential savings to taxpayers, yet they have been stymied in their work by an administration that rebuffs or delays the IGs' access to federal agency records.

- At the Environmental Protection Agency, the inspector general investigated allegations that the identities of several whistle-blowers within the Chemical Safety Board had been learned by the CSB's general counsel, Richard Loeb, exposing them to potential retaliation and contrary to regulations that require the Office of Special Counsel to protect whistle-blowers' identities. Loeb and CSB chairman Dr. Rafael Moure-Eraso then refused to cooperate with the IG's investigation of the leaks. In a repeat of a familiar pattern, Loeb cited attorney-client privilege and turned out to be conducting CSB business on personal email accounts to avoid scrutiny. IG Arthur Elkins reported the obstruction to Congress, and the committee held a hearing on June 19, 2014, to address both reprisals against whistle-blowers and general mismanagement at CSB. We concluded that Dr. Moure-Eraso lied to Congress in testimony before the Oversight Committee and the matter was referred to the Justice Department for prosecution in July 2015.

- Also at EPA, John Beale remained on the payroll for several years, doing little or no work while falsely claiming to be a CIA operative in need of secret cover. EPA was uncooperative with parts of the investigation. An attorney in EPA's Office of General Counsel declined to be interviewed about the matter by the IG despite being required by law to do so. At our committee hearing on May 7, 2014, a representative of the IG warned that because of the EPA's cover-up, his office "cannot assure the Committee that we are doing everything possible to root out other John Beales." The EPA IG also warned of obstruction by EPA's Office of

Homeland Security, Office of the Chief Financial Officer, Office of Chemical Safety and Pollution Prevention, and Office of General Counsel.

All of that happened during the watch of the head of the EPA, Gina McCarthy, who as of this writing, is still in the job.

- Sexual assaults were at the center of an investigation into the Peace Corps, where volunteers were reportedly attacked and officials withheld records about such assaults from the IG, in clear violation of the Kate Puzey Peace Corps Volunteer Protection Act of 2011, which requires the IG to track and report on such incidents. The Peace Corps audaciously argued that the Puzey Act overrode its older and more basic requirement in the Inspector General Act of 1978 to provide the IG all requested documents. The IG and the Peace Corps worked out an agreement allowing the IG restricted access to the relevant records, but such an arrangement should never have been necessary under the law.

- Another use of a relatively minor element of law as an impediment to older, more basic legal principles is the Department of Justice's assertion that the IG Act should now be interpreted to give its Office of Professional Responsibility jurisdiction over allegations of misconduct involving DOJ lawyers and law enforcement, potentially turning proceedings that should be conducted like criminal investigations into something more like internal human resources squabbles. This strategic move has prevented the IG looking into several controversies at DOJ, including the decision not to investigate possible voter intimidation by the New Black Panther Party, possible prosecutorial misconduct in the prosecution of Senator Ted Stevens (R-AK), and the drafting of memos advising the Bush White House on torture. The DOJ's IG would like to repeal the portion of the IG Act that yields its investigative powers to the Office of Professional Responsibility.

Lawyers can debate the details of the laws that created the Oversight Committee, Inspectors General, and special counsels. The broad incentives involved are common sense, though. Sufficiently emboldened bureaucrats, whether fueled by laziness, corruption, or real ideological conviction, will be least likely to listen to those investigators who have the least power to impose legal consequences on them. In the end, Oversight's power, unlike the special counsels', is mainly to shine a light on abuses and to shame the perpetrators.

For now, absent the power to arrest uncooperative witnesses and seize requested documents, in the disturbing cases in which the investigated appointees simply don't care whether they are in compliance with the law and don't care about the negative publicity, Oversight, for all it does to shape the political conversations of the day, is in a sense powerless. It also works with few resources and few staffers compared to the vast and powerful executive-branch bureaucracy on which it attempts to keep an eye. Even the IGs, with their greater resources, remain part of the executive branch they police and should not be the public's sole check on misconduct by executive-branch agencies.

Congress is the natural counterbalance to executive-branch overreach. The Oversight Committee is the natural instrument of congressional investigation into the executive branch. Legal penalties and the power to compel document release are the natural tools of such investigations. It is said that the legislative branch, and specifically the more populous House of Representatives, is the part of the federal government closest to the people. If the House is powerless to punish executive-branch wrongdoing, the people are powerless as well.

The temptation for the executive branch to misbehave grows if it becomes aware that the legislative branch will not respond. Superficially, the appearance is of a government without internal conflicts. In the long run, though, "absolute power corrupts absolutely." The Obama administration passes laws giving itself more and more power, grants itself more and more money, and then ignores legitimate attempts to question its actions. Sounds like absolute power to me.

Yet the Obama administration has repeatedly shown itself hostile toward the watchdogs, and that hostility did not build gradually.

In the very first year of Obama's presidency, the inspector general of AmeriCorps, Gerald Walpin, began investigating the mayor of Sacramento, Obama supporter and former NBA player Kevin Johnson, for misappropriating AmeriCorps funds. Obama fired Walpin.

Even the partisan Democrat Senator Claire McCaskill of Missouri questioned why a legally required explanation for Walpin's firing was not immediately given, leading to Obama's releasing a statement alleging that at a May 2009 meeting Walpin had been "confused, disoriented, and unable to answer questions and exhibited behavior that led the board to question his capacity to serve," leading the entire AmeriCorps board to call for Walpin's resignation.

Yet the approximately $850,000 that Johnson had encouraged the AmeriCorps board to give to his St. HOPE Academy was soon returned.

Obama also removed the acting inspector general of the International Trade Commission, Judith Gwynn, and left numerous inspector general posts vacant for years. One vacancy was at the State Department during the tenure of Hillary Clinton. Think her office could have used some independent oversight? Think it's a coincidence that it didn't have any?

The Obama administration's surprising lack of transparency, its vindictive attitude toward whistle-blowers, and its hostility to oversight in all its forms go hand in hand.

In response to this pattern of interference by the current administration, forty-seven inspectors general sent an unprecedented letter to Congress on August 5, 2014, describing "serious limitations on access to records that have recently impeded the work of Inspectors General."

If this is the first time you're learning of this, you're in considerable company. Almost in totality, the media took a startling pass on this story, and I've never understood why. The Obama administration's moves against independent review and internal oversight have been as serious as any "midnight massacre" that occurred during the Watergate scandal, with arguably wider implications.

The next president will likely face even stiffer resistance and more extensive oversight because additional congressional committees have established and been granted subpoena power. This is due in no small fact to the distribution of my former staff in other positions in the House and Senate, who have helped to spread the spirit of oversight. It's a very good sign for the future.

The public must also realize that they, too, have a stake in not tolerating these and other brazen acts to keep secret what should be known.

CHAPTER SIXTEEN

Taking the Administration to Court

One traditional explanation of the role of the three branches of government is that the legislature makes laws, the executive branch executes them, and the judiciary judges their constitutionality and hears cases when the laws are broken or in conflict.

What happens, though, when the relationship between the three branches devolves into one in which the legislature makes laws and the executive branch breaks them? Further, what happens when the executive branch grows so large that the regulations (and executive orders) it issues begin to outweigh in significance the lawmaking function of the legislature?

At some point, if the other two branches do nothing when an executive branch seizes the power to make rules—and do nothing when the officials of that same executive branch ignore or suspend those rules—we veer closer to rule by decree, if not by king, with more special deals for the well connected, more worried waiting by businesses that don't quite know what the law of the land will be from one month to the next.

To reassert law, Congress must give more thought to the mechanisms by which it can respond when an out-of-control executive branch goes astray. It does not have to act alone, nor should it simply override the wishes of the executive without deep consideration. It can do what most Americans do when they have a seemingly unresolvable dispute: take the matter to court.

The Founders, having recently fought a war against a king, were so wary of the presidency becoming overly powerful or demagogic that they did not even want the president to make routine direct addresses to the public, creating the institution of the State of the Union address as one way of keeping presidential communications directed to the legislature, the real center of political power. It was even considered controversial that Andrew Johnson went on a three-week speaking tour to promote his plan for Reconstruction.

Over the past century, Congress has delegated more and more responsibility to the president, so that today many of the rules by which we live are not laws made by Congress but regulations crafted by executive-branch agencies. Is it any surprise, really, that when President Obama issued his disastrously reckless executive order suspending many of the nation's immigration laws, he justified it by saying he could no longer wait for Congress to act the way he wished?

Many of the most familiar administrative agencies were created by Franklin Roosevelt's New Deal administration, including the Securities and Exchange Commission, the Federal Deposit Insurance Corporation, the Federal Communications Commission, and the Social Security Board, all bigger and more influential now, and wielding vast rule-making power without waiting for laws to be made.

In a further delegation of rule-making authority that makes real regulation yet another step removed from the public and from Congress, some of these regulatory agencies have grown complacent about the practice of "sue and settle" in which activist groups routinely sue them, arguing that the law demands more extreme action by the agency in pursuit of the activists' pet goals, such as stricter EPA regulations, and then negotiate behind closed doors for a regulatory solution agreeable to the activists *and the regulators*—not the public.

During Obama's first term, the EPA accounted for more of those cases than all other agencies combined by a factor of six, resulting in the creation of more than a hundred new regulations, with an estimated price tag of $100 million—each.

The EPA's eagerness to fold in the face of activist and litigious pressure has contributed to its reversing its own rulings in many cases, routinely imposing greater costs (and greater confusion) upon businesses in the process, with minimal increase in environmental benefits. EPA has revoked mining permits three years into major mining projects, dramatically but from a human health perspective pointlessly ratcheted up antimercury pollution rules, and expanded its authority to deny sensible permits under the Clean Water Act, all under pressure from activists.

The disturbing pattern here, though, is one in which activists encouraging government growth sometimes have far more influence on policy details than do the businesses and individual citizens who struggle to comply with the resulting regulations.

Though many activist groups portray themselves as system outsiders and critics of the government, they often rely on it for their funding. Consider the cozy relationship between the public-sector employees' union Service Employees International Union (SEIU) and progressive politicians such as Obama and New York City mayor Bill de Blasio and others whose programs pay their salaries, making them similarly foot soldiers of big government.

To supporters of big government, the weighing of new regulations is always quite efficient and rational, but regulations keep being added and few are ever repealed. In 2013, the economists John Dawson and Jon Seater estimated that the United States' annual output by the middle of the George W. Bush presidency was "about 28 percent of what it would have been had regulation remained at its 1949 level."[1] Are we living in a nation that is less than a third of what it might have been? How can we even begin to comprehend a policy error of that magnitude, with all the implications it has for people's quality of life, the pace of invention, lost jobs, and lost opportunity?

The government suing itself strikes some as absurd, but there is precedent for it. In fact, it has usually been Democrats who have brought such suits. The main basis for granting Congress the *standing* to sue in court has been different from the sort of standing granted to ordinary citizens to sue, though. An ordinary citizen— with far greater ease than Congress, really—can establish standing by showing that he has been materially harmed by inappropriate government action. Congress, by contrast, has usually brought suit, on the rare occasions it has asserted itself in this way, by arguing that its primary legal functions have been undermined and usurped by the executive. It is arguably easier for Congress to sue on the basis that the executive ought not to be de facto "legislating" *at all* (via regulations and executive orders) than it is to sue on the basis of the executive's policies being *bad ones* (though they often are, of course).

President Obama, perhaps more than any president in recent history, has lamented that he is saddled with a purportedly do-nothing Congress. "If Congress won't act, I will," as he put it on the topic of immigration reform (a statement that his critics understandably interpret to mean "If Congress won't act *the way I want it to*, I will act alone"). Massive policy changes, including the issuing of work visas by the Department of Homeland Security to millions of undocumented immigrants, call for legislative deliberation, not unilateral presidential action.

There is room for debate over the intended scope of presidents' executive orders. There is room for legitimate debate over whether the House can bring suit against a president without approval by the Senate. But every American ought to be troubled by the suggestion that it is bold, even heroic, for a president to go it alone and leave the legislature in the dust.

For that reason, in early 2014 Speaker Boehner led an effort to authorize Congress to bring suit against the president on the issue. The House passed the bill, and in theory the courts could decide the matter. This, at least, was something of a test case for the idea of suing an out-of-line executive, similar to a bill passed by the House the previous year authorizing a suit over the administration's arbitrary delays in implementing portions of Obamacare. The president may have initiated the recent massive changes to the United States' health care policies. That does not mean he personally retains power in perpetuity to decide which aspects of the ill-advised plan can be rolled out and when.

As a nation, we have seen this before: Woodrow Wilson's belief (one that has been repeated in different formulations by many liberals ever since) that the Constitution is an antiquated document not fully capable of addressing modern problems and later FDR's threat to pack the Supreme Court with new judges unless the Court accepted his creation of an array of New Deal agencies were both serious challenges to the role of the legislature and judiciary.

To many young people, the constitutional separation of powers must sound like an archaic thing, a hindrance preventing charismatic presidents from "getting the job done." The frustrations caused by watching legislative gridlock and inaction merely add to their desire to see laws overridden. Expecting the executive branch always to get its way—and denouncing the legal, constitutional, and congressional hurdles in its way as "obstructionism"—is a formula not for problem solving but for the breakdown of a nation of law and liberty.

If the thought of any current president acting unilaterally or lawlessly doesn't worry you, simply imagine a president of the opposite party behaving with as much leeway and ask yourself whether you would feel the same way. The question in the minds of the press and pundits should not be "How pushy should the Oversight Committee be?" but "How much lawlessness do you plan to tolerate in the executive branch, and what exactly is your plan for keeping an eye on it?"

Attorney David Rivkin and law professor Elizabeth Price Foley argued in favor of congressional standing to sue in the July 25, 2014, *Washington Post*. Of interest to advocates of the Oversight Committee's role, they specifically argued for the importance of defending the power of subpoena. When Congress is not itself injured by the executive's action, it may not have standing to sue, they wrote.

In numerous other cases, federal courts have recognized a single chamber's standing to assert institutional injury caused by the executive's refusal to comply with congressional subpoenas. In those cases, the chamber passed a resolution authorizing litigation to vindicate its institutional injury, which was described as a nullification of the chamber's investigatory power.

As the Supreme Court made clear in *Eastland v. United States Servicemen's Fund* in 1975, subpoenas are "inherent in the power to make laws" and an "integral part of the lawmaking process." A failure to comply with a chamber's subpoena, in other words, is an injury to the lawmaking power of the chamber itself. The institutional injury caused by the executive nullification of a subpoena is far less than that caused by the executive nullification of a law. If ignoring a congressional subpoena is sufficient to establish legislative standing, ignoring a law should be more than sufficient as well.

That's a start. It's sad, perhaps, that instead of directly legislating to right wrongs in society or shore up the basic principles of property, we're reduced to this approach several times removed from that: contemplating filing a lawsuit aimed, really, at getting the judicial branch to compel the executive merely to respond to prior questions and document requests about possible wrongdoing.

The courts have historically been reluctant to grant Congress standing, but the stronger and more presumptuous the executive branch grows, and the more accustomed the legislature and judiciary become to passivity in the face of that strength, the more congressional standing to sue is needed. Even for the executive branch, there must at least be the possibility of legal consequences or Congress really will have become a legislature in name only.

But we ought to be able to agree in a bipartisan—or rather nonpartisan—fashion that when crimes are committed, laws flouted, records hidden or altered, or the public trust otherwise violated, Congress should retain at the very least the right to ask questions of the executive, and the right at least to have its case heard before the judiciary if the executive refuses to cooperate. I cannot imagine a business long enduring that walled itself off from criticism the way government agencies would like to wall themselves off from the public and its representatives.

One such business that suffered terribly as a result of unfair government action was the national arts and crafts chain Hobby Lobby, which had to go all the way to the Supreme Court to litigate its right not to provide—against its religious beliefs—certain drugs and devices in the company's health insurance plan.

This is not to take sides in a dispute over whether to agree or not with Hobby Lobby's policies, but their rights in the circumstance were obvious—and obviously violated. Congress specifically wrote a religious exemption into the Obamacare law *at the insistence of several Democrats*, and the Obama administration ignored that law as it acted against Hobby Lobby.

Ultimately, the company defended its rights and prevailed in the high court. But why did it have to go that far? In my view, the Obama administration violated a specific law of Congress as well as its clear legislative intent, and we had to watch as one brave company was forced to use its own time and resources to stand up to the government as it sought to intimidate as much as litigate.

We should have supported Hobby Lobby—and others who are in the right—and said to the White House: *pick on someone your own size.*

Americans are an optimistic, problem-solving people—but one side effect of those characteristics is seeing things in need of improvement everywhere. Transforming—and regulating—every aspect of our lives is not, however, a path to a "great society." It's a path toward totalitarianism, especially when unchecked by other parts of government. Regulation is now everywhere in our lives, and if it is administered in a politicized, arbitrary, legally unconstrained fashion—if the appointees who do the regulating do not answer to lawmakers—we will have surrendered our democracy and our liberty.

CHAPTER SEVENTEEN

The Only Good Government Is Open Government

I have been fortunate, starting from fairly ordinary beginnings and finding success in both business and politics. Though I think it is important for government not to make all our choices for us and provide for all our wants, I can sympathize with the many Americans who feel as if something beyond their control, both economic and political, has been shaping their destiny—especially in the years since the financial crisis began. The populist rumblings on both the far right and far left sometimes take anticapitalist forms, but there is also something Jeffersonian about them, a longing across the political spectrum for average citizens to make a difference instead of feeling like pawns of the elite and the well connected. Transparency and oversight do not guarantee that the system will give each of us what we want, but they at least give citizens some hope of knowing what's going on.

The quest for open government is no marginal issue. My belief in the necessity of the DATA Act was heightened by Treasury Secretary

Geithner testifying before Congress that the government couldn't track the TARP bailout funds—while private-sector analysts told us it was not only possible but had been done for years in the private sector.

Admittedly, democracy and openness are not always efficient. But despite its flaws, we bet on democracy when we founded the nation, and we should bet on transparency now. Not only because we hope democracy will yield good results and keep government tethered to the will of the public but because we know that a government cloaked in secrecy, even one that makes efficient decisions today, cannot be trusted always to do so in the future. Just as a government without checks on executive power grows corrupt, so, too, does a government without transparency grow accustomed to ignoring its citizens by viewing public information as a hindrance and a nuisance, something to be gotten around, not enthusiastically embraced.

Realistically, though, a government insulated from scrutiny, criticism, and legal consequences will not long be attentive to its own failures. If we cannot easily see what is wrong and hold accountable officials who have made mistakes, it is difficult to encourage policy reform. Transparency and efficiency, then, go together more often than not, rather than being at odds—so long as there are consequences for mistakes. Combine such incentives with an active, engaged legislature, and there might yet be hope of restoring a republic capable of routine course corrections. It won't be the dynamism of the marketplace, but it would be a start.

The real future of oversight isn't with an official committee of twelve or fifteen or even fifteen hundred elected officials. The future of oversight is with the public and through access to government information so that both individuals and groups of people are free to peruse that information and dissect it many times over.

It is not only the most efficient way nor the only practical way, but also the most meaningful and effective way to empower citizens.

I entered public life holding two fundamental beliefs: that government is too big and taxes are too high. All these years later, I feel the same way, if not more so.

I've been a tough critic of the federal bureaucracy and the encroaching power of the public sector—and at times I've been even tougher than that. The things I've seen done in the name of the government range from foolish to wrong to downright immoral.

But service in Congress has been the great honor of my life. And I'm proud of what I've done in public government service. So my criticisms of government come from wanting to reform it and make it better. And I'm as concerned as I am critical, for with its current size, structure, and standpoint, making government great is not possible.

We need smaller government. And we need smarter government. But what we can achieve first—that will help get us there—is *open government.*

Government has proved itself consistently resistant to political pressure, to public criticism, even to court orders and clear law. So it will require something more potent and new tools to truly transform what government is and how it impacts the lives of every American.

That's where I believe technology can make the decisive difference.

When I started my own business, I did not set out to create a technology enterprise; I just set out to start a business. It could have been manufacturing floor tile, assembling baseball gloves, or constructing office furniture. By good fortune, I happened onto the technology world, and I've spent the better part of the last four decades fascinated by what it can do and what it can deliver.

Technology is a constant driver of change and a permanent innovator of reform. Because it is derived from both dreams and discoveries, it must always go forward. It can never reverse. And the march of technology will continue to get better, faster, and more accessible as long as consumers demand it.

Technology has helped us communicate in almost limitless ways at lightning speed. It has provided new ways to work on our own terms and on our own time. It has allowed us to live better and longer.

If it can do all that, why can't it open government to improve government?

The answer is that it can, but only as a tool. The hands that utilize this tool belong solely and only to the people.

Technology is the ideal gateway to an open government that encourages citizen engagement and allows the public to see, shape, and understand its system of laws, rules, and regulations.

We need to create a government that works as intended and works hard for its money. We need a system that delivers true value by allowing access to its information, enabling an impact on its lawmaking, and shortening the distance between people and the government.

Much has been written about today's "wired world" and "Facebook and Twitter revolutions," and that is certainly true as it impacts people's individual lives. We've never been more virtually connected.

But spend a few days amid Washington's lobbying culture, on Capitol Hill, or in the middle floors of an enormous federal agency building, and the only common sensation will be isolation from the outside world.

We've never needed open government more.

This cause exploded onto the Washington scene in the short but furious fight in late 2011 over the Stop Online Piracy Act—a laudable goal, to be sure, but the legislation in question would have harmed the free flow of the Internet itself.

The bill was authored and advanced by Hollywood, the recording industry, and large publishers as a solution to piracy—which is a serious problem. Given its powerful backers, it was moving quickly and nothing was going to stop it.

But many of us on both sides of the aisle, including Google, Facebook, Twitter, Wikipedia, and Reddit, understood quickly that the bill would stifle the Web by legally compelling social media companies and search engines to serve as an enforcement arm of the Department of Justice.

Eventually, some of the most prominent websites in the world "went dark" for a day to highlight what was at stake. Wikipedia, for example, suspended its popular website for twenty-four hours and posted only this solemn warning against a blacked-out screen:

IMAGINE A WORLD WITHOUT FREE KNOWLEDGE

For over a decade, we have spent millions of hours building the largest encyclopedia in human history. Right now, the U.S. Congress is considering legislation that could fatally damage the free and open Internet. For 24 hours, we are blacking out Wikipedia.

Fundamentally, I was opposed, based on the simple principle of wanting to keep the Web open. Nothing has brought more prosperity and more innovation to the four corners of our planet, and if allowed to flourish, it can reach even more deeply. But only an open Internet can do that. And only an open government can guarantee it.

The battle was joined in the House Judiciary Committee, chaired by my friend Lamar Smith (R-TX), who was all for SOPA. He is a fair and thoughtful man, and he has my respect. But he was mistaken, and he was wise to recognize quickly that opposition to his bill was serious—and growing. Those of us opposed were gaining momentum but were overmatched in a conventional Washington-style contest.

So we opened up the process by inviting in everybody in the world to watch and weigh in.

My office organized and launched keepthewebopen.com, a website anyone could access that streamed the video feed of the hearing and combined it with a copy of all legislation and text, along with an area for commentary from anyone watching.

On day one, more than 138,000 American web users watched the hearing on our site. By comparison, when more than two hundred people attempted to watch the live stream on the Judiciary Committee's site—it crashed.

KeepTheWeb#OPEN allowed everyone to watch and follow and understand what was happening live. Tens of thousands of people posted their opinions in their own words. Some even suggested substitute legislative language, amendments, and clarification. It was a prairie fire of public access. All we did was let people see.

Everyone in Congress was aware of what was happening, and several members of the House and Senate, even sponsors of the legislation, withdrew their support. That led directly to the derailing of SOPA.

But more than the fact that we were stopping a bad idea, it felt right because it was the right thing to do. I could not help but think at the time: this is the way we should be doing our jobs.

Those 138,000 Americans went to our website because they cared about what we were doing, believed it was important to follow the process, and then lent their voices to the debate. That's what carried the day. Why can't that happen every time?

I absolutely believe that government can serve the citizens better while spending less and growing smaller. And given the exceptionally low esteem in which the vast majority of the public now holds the government, my view is: it will have to. You can't fix or improve something you have no respect for. The day the American people stop believing they have the power to stop, start, or change their government is the day a part of this country dies.

Opening government and welcoming both a closer look and consistent input (as well as criticism) from as many people as possible can go a long way to restoring and earning the respect of the people.

CHAPTER EIGHTEEN

Looking Back, Moving Ahead

When we began our investigation into the 2012 attacks on the US diplomatic compound in Benghazi, I never imagined it would reveal the existence of Hillary Clinton's private email server, her back-channel network of shady contacts, or the clear conflicts of interest that she put into place practically from day one of her tenure as secretary of state.

Clinton has blamed anyone and everyone on her long and growing enemies list, but if she is genuinely interested in identifying what unraveled her public image and undermined her personal credibility, she need look no further than the truth. For it is true that she violated every fundamental standard of public disclosure, mishandled top secret and confidential national security information, and wouldn't come clean when it came to light.

If she had been anywhere near as careful to protect the United States' secrets as she was her own, we would have been in better hands.

Though I do not know what the political destiny of Hillary Clinton will be, I can say with certainty that if she reaches the White House, we will have truly turned a corner—straight into a dead end where politicians can do pretty much as they please, when they please, without your knowing much more than that you get to pay for it all.

Though it was certainly a surprise to find out five years into the Obama administration how unreliable his State Department had been, it really shouldn't have come as a shock. Since it began, the Obama administration has dedicated itself to increasing government power, practicing media spin and political cover-up. The result has been terrible damage to the institution of the presidency and the reputation of the executive branch.

Again and again since 2009, the Congress as an institution and the Oversight Committee as Congress's instrument have been compelled to cope with a situation that our system of government is at present unprepared to solve: abuse of power by the executive branch, enabled by an amorphous bureaucracy that denies the people's right to know.

The Obama and Clinton deceptions went far beyond conventional partisan politics and exposed something deeper and more troubling in the fabric of Washington. Though some in my party fervently opposed President Obama and his fellow Democrats defended everything he did, the White House response wasn't to ease these tensions but to exacerbate them. That perpetuated the real problem, which is deeper than partisanship: our chronic, systemic, and profound lack of accountability combined with the politicians' innate instinct to refuse responsibility and shift blame.

I've met President Obama several times but don't know him personally. As his presidency ends, we know his manner all too well, though. Whatever his intelligence and abilities—and they are considerable—I believe he will leave office a substantially different person and will leave the nation's capital a dramatically different place than when he moved into the White House in 2009.

Some Obama supporters lament that after the great expectations of hope and change, his administration didn't change Washington very much. But that's not true. The Obama administration has indeed changed Washington. It's made it worse.

Rather than healing and building consensus, President Obama set out to rule by fiat and to dictate rather than persuade. When the voters threw the Democrats out of the majority and handed the House of Representatives to the GOP in a 2010 landslide, they did so in no small part because the House had behaved as if it were Obama's palace guard.

Though the president was reelected with 51 percent of the vote in 2012, after more of the same misbehavior, the voters flipped the US Senate to Republican control, too. So controversial was the president in his second term that in some of the senatorial elections of 2014, the Democratic candidates would not even admit to having voted for Obama in 2012.

This is not because the voters have fundamentally changed what's in their hearts but because they changed their minds. Obama and his team have been too partisan, too divisive, too dismissive, and too determined to deny accountability. As a result, the branches of government are constantly at war over things as basic as access to public information and as fundamental as the truth about how Americans got killed defending our Benghazi compound and our southern border with Mexico. Surely there is enough to argue about without destroying all semblance of American consensus.

Obama's 2008 pledge that his would be the "most transparent administration in history" was worse than an empty campaign boast or act of self-serving glibness; it was the cloak concealing a calculated move *against* transparency, a manipulation not only of his core supporters but also of all fair and open-minded Americans who were willing to offer their trust.

Obama's promise that "If you like your doctor, you can keep your doctor. Period," for instance, was worse than the conventional pie-in-the-sky sop to voters in an election year that might not have worked as well as hoped. Voters expect those. It was a central assurance to millions of concerned Americans that he knew wasn't true and never would be.

Obama's pronouncement that there wasn't "a smidgen" of corruption at the IRS was worse than a colloquial dismissal of mountains of evidence and months of public disclosure. It was a sneering, scornful disdain for the real suffering that people were experiencing at the hands of his appointees, regardless of whether he had ordered it.

Obama may believe he was helped politically by his message discipline and disavowal of what came to be widely known about Obamacare, Fast and Furious, Benghazi, the IRS, and so much else. After all, he and his fellow Democrats did not endorse our findings, thereby denying us a bipartisan seal of approval on the apparent record of wrongdoing. His repeated false assertions may have rendered ambiguous the official verdict on his administration's deceptions, but the majority of the country now knows the fundamental facts and has repeatedly held him and his party politically responsible.

This is one reason Obama has fallen from stratospheric heights of public approval in 2009 to the marginally unpopular place he occupies today. I very much doubt that the president's unpopularity—or the president himself—will change until after he leaves office. That is a great shame. It did not have to be this way.

There are, as of this writing, eighty-three fewer Democrats in Congress than on the day Obama was sworn into office. Many of them I worked with, some of them I liked personally, but most of them were no doubt sacrificed to the White House's round-the-clock politicking and the deep rifts it has caused in this country.

The voters invested much hope and many votes in this president and his party, and they've been making consistent withdrawals at the ballot box ever since. Though Republicans have been the fortunate recipients of those second thoughts, we have yet to convince as many as we should that the GOP is truly deserving of that windfall.

When I entered Congress, I was told that every new member looks to the legislator on the left and then the one to the right and wonders how he or she ever came to be among such giants. Soon after—the adage goes—you again look to the colleague on the left and then the one to the right and wonder how they could have been elected at all. Irony notwithstanding, nothing moves a person to feel like an outsider among government elites than several years on the inside.

But even as I have become all too aware of the human flaws and systemic problems of our government, motivating me through all of this has been the hope that we can still make our government worthy of the inventive, creative, and resourceful Americans it was designed to serve. We have a lot of repair work to do.

One cause for optimism is that the march of technology and innovation is poised to overwhelm government's use of outdated, user-unfriendly processes. One reason I authored the DATA Act, and a reason it attracted bipartisan support, is that it will not simply modernize government's systems, it will help make them easily accessible by every single American.

Imagine if we used technology to go beyond the Freedom of Information Act. Every day, countless individuals, companies, news organizations, and legal services try to get information under FOIA. And every one of those requests has to be processed and examined by a person, not a program. The delays can be extensive and, as a result, expensive. It's a waste of time, money, and our national potential.

Imagine if seeking public information were like searching Google, rather than like hunting for a needle in a haystack. Imagine if all the spending in nonclassified government contracts to all of the government's vendors were made open and available. Imagine how quickly we could find out that the government, perhaps through mistake rather than intention, had paid ten different prices for the same product. This would not only increase the value of government services, it would earn government a measure of credibility now so utterly lacking in the eyes of Americans.

Our political problems are deep, but most of them are not new. Though I am a proud and loyal Republican, I know that neither just electing more Republicans nor bland calls for "bipartisanship" will solve anything. Indeed, between some parts of government— for example, between those performing oversight and those being investigated—there *ought* to be an adversarial relationship.

Members of Congress should be united, though, when an administration resists oversight. On this, my views have evolved.

My colleagues have every right to disagree about whether an administration should be investigated, and they can be divided about what the results of an investigation may reveal. But when a committee of Congress issues a legal request for information, it is absolutely essential that we realize it isn't being done in the name of Republicans, Democrats, the *New York Times*, or Fox News; it's being done in the name of the American people.

The most important difference any of us can make at this precarious moment in the nation's history is to remind government that it is still subject to the rule of law and still expected to meet a strictest standard of accountability. The task of oversight, in a democracy, belongs to all of us.

Oversight, after all, is not just about highlighting past abuses. It is about preventing future ones.

Oversight is the people's view—and Washington's watchdog. It's the light that pierces the dark and shines brightly into concealed corners. It's the breaking down of the stonewall and the clearing of the smokescreen. It's the cracking of the code that conceals things you should know. It's the citizen's voice that's often ignored, yet still asks, "How could this happen?"

Oversight is the fundamental right of all Americans to know as much about their government as their government knows about them. It's the first line of defense against retribution for speaking the truth and the last word that tells us the best and worst of what our leaders have done. Oversight is the need to know and the need to act.

Oversight is standing up for the innocent victims the IRS worked to deny and sought to destroy. It's helping the family of Brian Terry wanting to know why he died, being lied to by the Justice Department, and having nowhere else to turn. It's remembering the families of the fallen in Benghazi, learning from our investigation the terrible truth of what had happened to our people and the shocking lies told in the service of White House damage control.

Oversight is all these things. It is worth the effort. And it is worth the fight.

Acknowledgments

This is a tribute to many people: some known, mostly unknown, and a few even anonymous.

The staff of the House Oversight and Government Reform Committee performed splendidly throughout every stage of the extraordinarily difficult burden that was often theirs alone to bear. From start to finish, and often from dawn until well past midnight, they drove our search for the truth and carried the cause of accountability. At all times, they were as creative, resolute, and entrepreneurial as anyone I've witnessed in the private sector—and often far more resourceful.

The Inspectors General have perhaps Washington's most thankless job: they are the in-house watchdogs of the executive branch, charged with rooting out wrongdoing; they also have the isolation, exclusion, and even derision that often go with it. They are uncommonly courageous, continuing to press forward while knowing full well they could be risking their careers and even their families' well-being. They are unsung heroes, gallant and determined professionals, and we need them now more than ever.

Finally, to the thousands of dedicated professionals who work at all levels of our federal government, truly care about what they do, and serve with a higher purpose. Often derided as the "Washington bureaucracy," they are, instead, an indispensable resource of institutional knowledge. I am deeply grateful to all the people who did their job and came forward to tell the truth. It was the right thing to do. And it made all the difference.

A personal note: I wrote this book with the help and assistance of family, friends, colleagues, associates, and even strangers who spoke with me in airports, coffee shops, and countless other places where I was lucky enough to meet them, listen to their concerns, and receive their good wishes.

Like any wise man, I am first and always thankful to my family for the strength, support, and uncommon spirit that bring cherished purpose to our lives.

Finally, I am particularly grateful to the following:

Dale Neugebauer
Larry Brady
Frederick Hill
Steve Castor
Mark Marin
John Cuaderes
Christoper Hixon
Ashok Pinto
Becca Watkins
Rob Borden
Peter Warren
Tyler Grimm
Adam Fromm
Molly Boyl
Seamus Kraft
Justin LoFranco
Phil Paule
and Jonathan Wilcox

Endnotes

Chapter Seven: Second Thoughts on Six Years with the Fourth Estate

1. Cristina Corbin, "ACORN to Play Role in 2010 Census," Fox News, March 18, 2009, http://www.foxnews.com/politics/2009/03/18/acorn-play-role-census.html.

2. "ACORN Workers Caught on Tape Allegedly Advising on Prostitution," CNN, September 11, 2009, http://www.cnn.com/2009/POLITICS/09/10/acorn.prostitution/.

Chapter Eight: Fast and Furious

1. Al Kamen and Sari Horwitz, "Holder Fast and Furious E-mail Talks about 'Issa and His Idiot Cronies,'" *Washington Post*, November 4, 2014, https://www.washingtonpost.com/blogs/in-the-loop/wp/2014/11/04/holder-fast-and-furious-e-mail-talks-about-issa-and-his-idiot-cronies/.

Chapter Nine: The Difference Benghazi Makes

1. "Press Briefing by Press Secretary Jay Carney, 9/14/2012," September 14, 2012, https://www.whitehouse.gov/the-press-office/2012/09/14/press-briefing-press-secretary-jay-carney-9142012.

2. "Ambassador Rice: Benghazi Attack Began Spontaneously," NBC, September 16, 2012, http://usnews.nbcnews.com/_news/2012/09/16/13896494-ambassador-rice-benghazi-attack-began-spontaneously.

3. "Flashback: What Susan Rice Said about Benghazi," *Wall Street Journal*, November 16, 2012, http://blogs.wsj.com/washwire/2012/11/16/flashback-what-susan-rice-said-about-benghazi/.

Chapter Ten: Lois Lerner: The Power to Tax and the Power to Destroy

1. John Sexton, "Lois Lerner Discusses Political Pressure on IRS in 2010," YouTube, August 6, 2013, https://www.youtube.com/watch?v=EH1ZRyq-1iM.

2. Stan Veuger, "Crashed IRS Computers as Likely as a Unicorn Eating Lois Lerner's E-mails," American Enterprise Institute, June 25, 2014, http://www.aei.org/publication/crashed-irs-computers-as-likely-as-a-unicorn-eating-lois-lerners-e-mails/print/.

3. Rick Hazen, "Transcript of Lois Lerner's Remarks at Tax Meeting Sparking IRS Controversy," Election Law Blog, May 11, 2013, https://electionlawblog.org/?p=50160.

4. Statement by the President, May 15, 2013, https://www.whitehouse.gov/the-press-office/2013/05/15/statement-president.

5. http://oversight.house.gov/wp-content/uploads/2014/07/Lerner-email-use-2.pdf.

6. https://oversight.house.gov/wp-content/uploads/2015/10/1027-Impeachment-Resolution.pdf, p. 46.

7. Ibid., p. 47.

8. http://democrats.oversight.house.gov/sites/democrats.oversight.house.gov/files/documents/2015-10-23%20DOJ%20to%20HOGR%20%28IRS%29%20-%20Chmn%20Chaffetz%20RM%20Cummings.pdf.

9. Treasury Inspector General for Tax Administration, "Inappropriate Criteria Were Used to Identify Tax-Exempt Applications for Review," May 14, 2013, https://www.washingtonpost.com/blogs/wonkblog/files/2013/05/201310053fr-revised-redacted-1.pdf?tid=a_inl.

10. Cleta Mitchell, "How Congress Botched the IRS Probe," *Wall Street Journal*, May 14, 2015, http://www.wsj.com/articles/how-congress-botched-the-irs-probe-1431645154.

Chapter Eleven: Hillary's Got a Secret (Email Server)

1. Anne Gearan, "Latest State Release: Clinton Emails with Chelsea after Benghazi Attacks and More," *Washington Post*, January 8, 2016, https://www.washingtonpost.com/news/post-politics/

wp/2016/01/08/with-2-a-m-state-department-email-trove-82-
percent-of-clinton-emails-now-released/.

Chapter Twelve: Bank Accounts as Political Weapons

1. "Financial Fraud Enforcement Task Force Executive Director
   Michael J. Bresnick at the Exchequer Club of Washington, D.C.,"
   https://www.justice.gov/opa/speech/financial-fraud-enforcement-
   task-force-executive-director-michael-j-bresnick-exchequer.

2. William Isaac, "DOJ Memo Leaves No Doubt about Choke
   Point's Motives," *American Banker*, July 18, 2014, http://www.
   americanbanker.com/bankthink/doj-memo-leaves-no-doubt-
   about-choke-points-motives-1068828-1.html.

3. "Bipartisan Members of Oversight Panel Urge Treasury to Return
   Seized Assets to Small Businesses," August 12, 2015, http://
   waysandmeans.house.gov/bipartisan-members-of-oversight-
   panel-urge-treasury-to-return-seized-assets-to-small-businesses/.

4. "IRS Apologizes for Seizing Bank Accounts of Small Businesses,"
   February 11, 2015, http://www.latimes.com/business/la-fi-irs-
   seizures-20150212-story.html.

5. "FDIC Chairman Comes under Fire during 'Operation Choke
   Point' Hearings," March 24, 2015, http://www.foxnews.com/
   politics/2015/03/24/fdic-chairman-comes-under-fire-during-
   operation-choke-point-hearings.html.

6. FDIC, "Guidance on Payment Processor Relationships,"
   November 7, 2008, http://ithandbook.ffiec.gov/media/28087/fdi-
   fil1272008.pdf.

7. Glenn Harlan Reynolds, "Justice Department Shuts Down Porn
   Money," *USA Today*, May 26, 2014, http://www.usatoday.com/
   story/opinion/2014/05/26/justice-department-porn-stars-first-
   amendment-column/9594113/.

Chapter Fourteen: Turning a Deaf Ear to Whistle-blowers and a Blind Eye to Cover-ups

1. "Is Obama Admin Threatening Benghazi Whistleblowers?,"
   April 29, 2013, http://insider.foxnews.com/2013/04/29/benghazi-
   threats-against-whistleblowers-alleged.

Chapter Fifteen: Why the Oversight Committee Keeps Watch

1. *Watkins v. United States*, 354 U.S. 178, June 17, 1957, https://www.law.cornell.edu/supremecourt/text/354/178#writing-USSC_CR_0354_0178_ZO.

2. Committee on House Administration, "Rules of the Committee on House Administration—114th Congress," https://cha.house.gov/about/rules-committee-house-administration.

Chapter Sixteen: Taking the Administration to Court

1. John W. Dawson and John J. Seater, "Federal Regulation and Aggregate Economic Growth," *Journal of Economic Growth*, January 2013, http://www4.ncsu.edu/~jjseater/regulationandgrowth.pdf, p. 2.